My Father Was a Farmer in New Cumnock

My Father Was a Farmer in New Cumnock

The story of a Scottish farming family

IAIN BAIRD

The Choir Press

First published in the United Kingdom in 2018 by
The Choir Press

ISBN 978-1-911589-96-9

Contents

Introduction

This story is about a farmer in the west of Scotland at the end of the nineteenth century. His name was John Baird and he was my great-grandfather. The members of the Baird family, who form the basis of this story, were real people whose lives I have researched to the best of my efforts. I have taken scraps of stories that were passed down through my family and used them to create the various scenarios in this book. Using an excellent description of the history of New Cumnock, *New Cumnock: Far and Away*, written by George Sanderson, and other historical references, I have speculated on how these historical events might have impacted on John and Flora Baird, and on the other family members who lived and loved in this Ayrshire community.

My second cousin lives in New Cumnock, as has his family for a number of generations. He gave me a Bible that had belonged to my great-grandfather, John. John had written his name in beautiful copperplate handwriting in the front leaf, along with a reference to Proverbs chapter 22, verse 1. This verse states:

> *A good name is rather to be chosen than great riches,*
> *and loving favour rather than gold and silver.*
>
> Proverbs 22.1

Through this simple Biblical reference I have made assumptions about John's beliefs, his character and his ideals. I have made similar assumptions, based on the family stories that have been passed down, about the characters of the children who grew up at the family farm, Meikle Garclaugh, and particularly my own grandfather, John James Baird.

I have described farming activities that are very likely to have taken place at Meikle Garclaugh, such as threshing corn with a steam-driven thresher, in order to provide some appropriate background to farming life in these times. Researching the weather in Scotland at the end of the nineteenth century made me realise what dreadful conditions farmers had to suffer during a decade of exceptionally cold years. These harsh periods are included within this story, along with their possible impact on the family.

In order to be able to tell the story of the Baird family I have created fictional characters and woven them into the true events that were taking place at that time. For instance, Richard Robertson is loosely based on a doctor who lived in New Cumnock at the time, but other than that he, his wife and his family are all fictional.

Robert Iain Baird
March 2018

Acknowledgements

My special thanks go to the following people for helping me write this story.

My wife, Jane Baird, for her encouragement and patience.

Andy Howat, for his valuable help with research around New Cumnock.

Mary Baird, my aunt, for providing me with a wealth of family stories.

Barbara Baird, my cousin, for providing useful family stories.

Anne Remmington, my good friend who always gives honest feedback.

The aunts, uncles and cousins who I have pestered for family information over thirty years or more.

Members of the Dean Writers Circle for their valuable advice.

My friends and family who have helped with proofreading and encouragement.

The Baird Family Trees

At Meikle Garclaugh

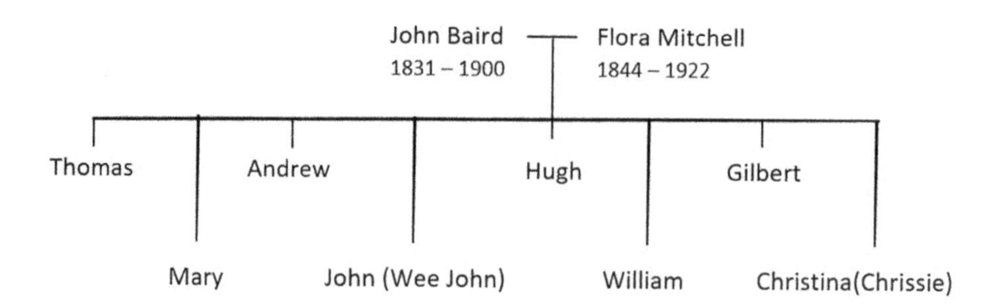

At South Blairkip

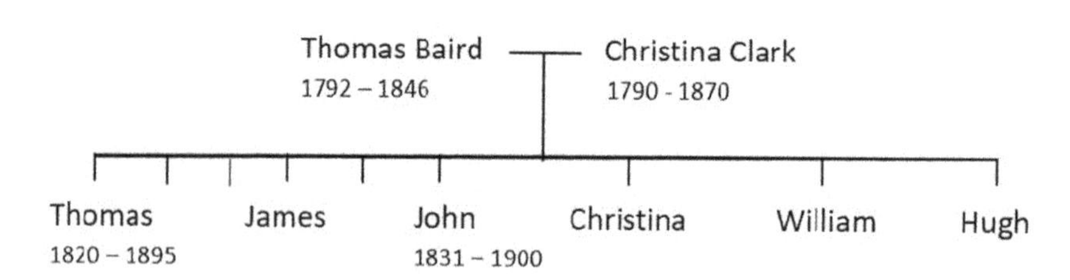

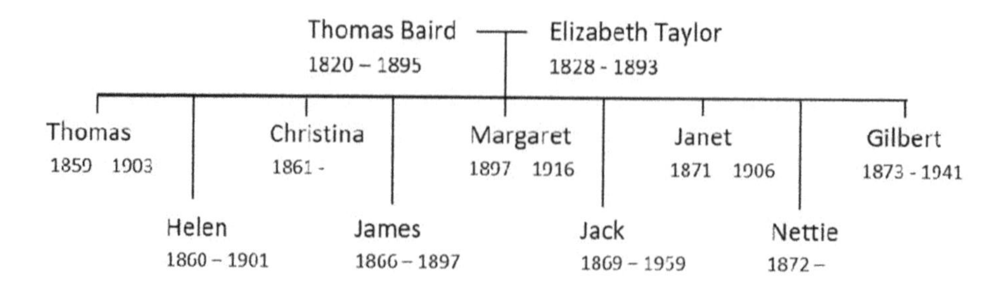

Maps

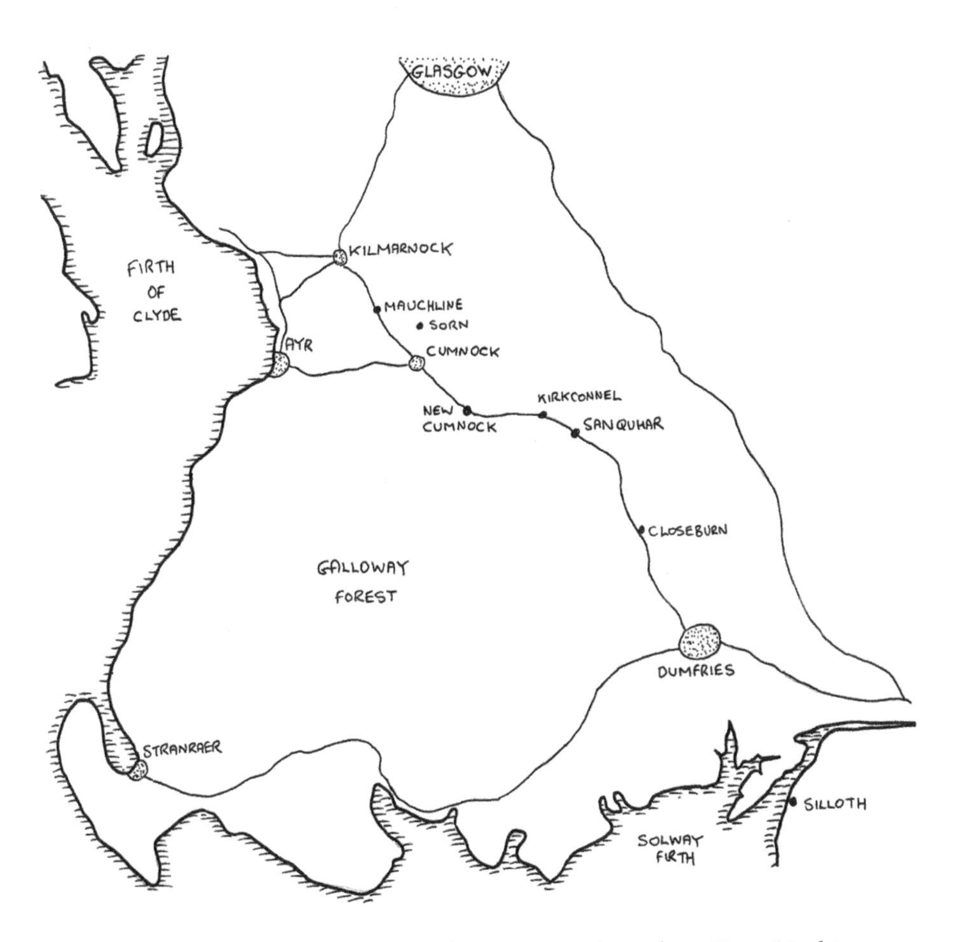

South West Scotland, showing the counties of Ayrshire, Dumfrieshire and Lanarkshire.

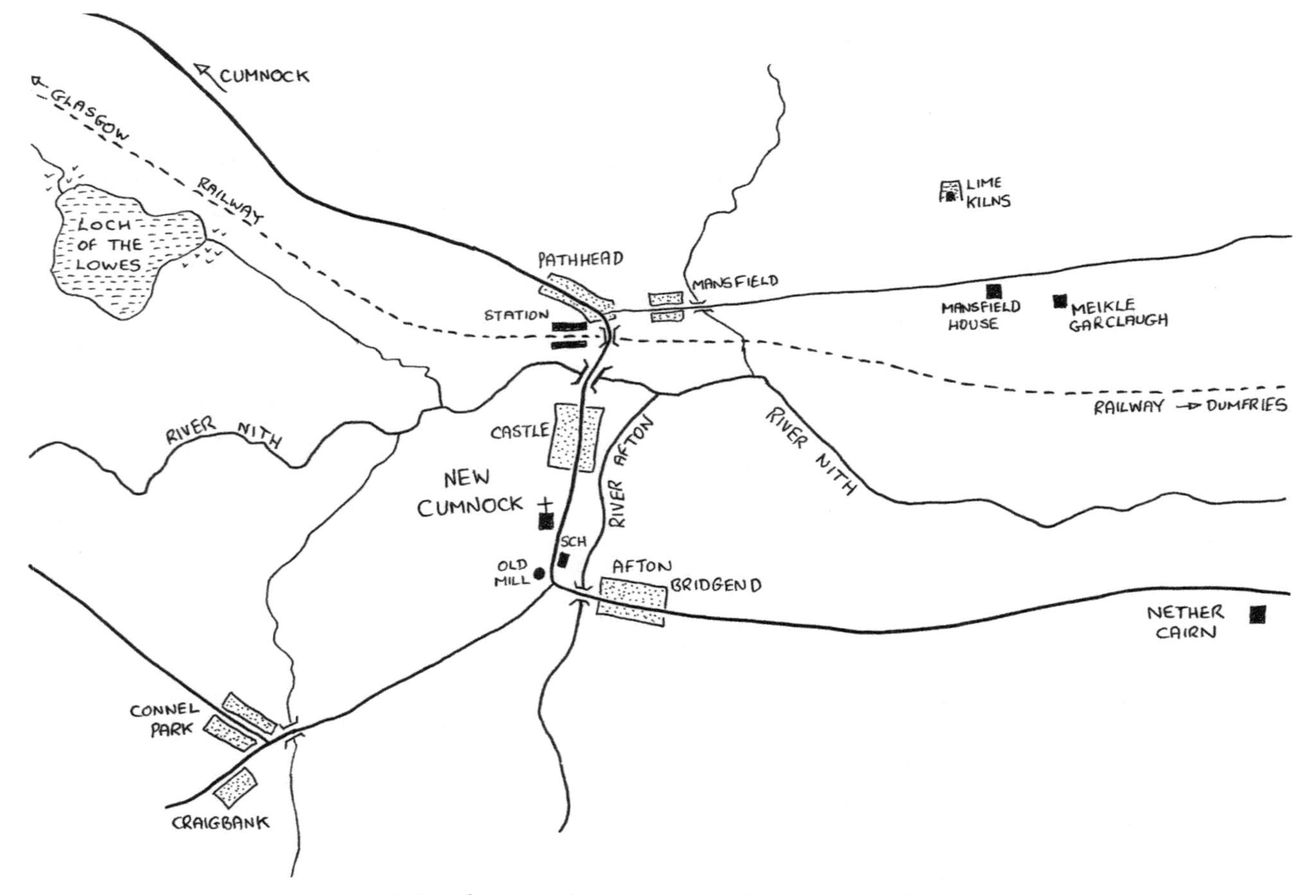

Map showing the area around New Cumnock.

Glossary

bairn	baby
bannock	small cake
blether	talk, gossip
bothy	alcohol drinking house
braw	beautiful
break	shooting break, horse-drawn transport
breeksbye	trouserswell (as an exclamation), or gosh.
byre	cattle shed
canny	clever, wise
chesset	cheese press
cludgie	toilet
conies	rabbits
coos	cows
courses	menstruation
doon	down
dunt	hit or bump
factor	estate manager
fettle	condition, vigour
howdie	midwife
ken	know
kirk	church
laird	landowner of a large estate
luggie	wooden bowl with handles on each side
meikle	large
mind	remember, worry
mingin	smelly
murrain	old name for contagious cattle diseases
neeps	turnips
rennet	enzyme used to separate curds from whey
rick	large stack of hay or corn

sheugh	field drainage ditch
steading	collection of farm buildings
stooks	a small stack of sheaves of corn
tablet	hard fudge sweet
tawpie	fool
tawse	leather punishment strap
twa	two
vittles'	food
wain	child
yen	one
ye	you

CHAPTER ONE
April 1869

Richard Robertson had left his seat in the carriage and was now on the platform at New Cumnock station. He stood next to his suitcase and his shiny new leather doctor's bag, surveying the scene. As the train had squealed and puffed to a stop in the station, the platform had quickly transformed itself into a bustle of activity. Richard soon found himself surrounded by this bustle of expectant passengers disembarking, onward travellers seeking out compartments for their own journeys and the ever-busy railway staff scurrying around the platform on their various tasks. At the end of the train, closer to the bridge over the railway tracks, goods were being hurriedly loaded and unloaded by porters, chivvied by the silent frown on the station master's face, his impatient watch in hand and its long chain swinging across to his black waistcoat like a pendulum. At the top end of the train the locomotive hissed steam, sounding like an exhausted plough-horse at the end of a furrow. The driver was inspecting the wheels of the green locomotive, disappearing and then reappearing as the clouds of steam drifted around him.

Richard gazed down the length of the platform, beyond the bridge that took the main road over the rail tracks. On either side of the Nith valley rose the mounds of the hills, green with the fresh flush of grass that had been dragged from its winter slumbers by an unusually warm February. Clusters of white clouds hurried across the blue sky, changing shape like the steam that floated around the locomotive.

'Can I give you a lift into toon, sir?'

A voice brought Richard out of his daydream. He looked down at a small man in brown and weathered clothes who was standing with his flat hat crunched in his hands, looking expectantly at him.

'Oh, yes. Yes, please,' Richard stuttered in reply. He bent to pick up his suitcase, but the man quickly stepped forward to beat him to the handle.

'And where would you be wanting to go, young sir?' the man asked, turning to walk briskly along the platform, which had now nearly emptied of people.

'Could you take me to Dr Cluny's surgery, please?' Richard called after the retreating figure.

'Nae problem, sir. Just follow me to the break.'

Richard increased his pace to keep up with the small man, who walked surprisingly quickly. They passed between the waiting room and the station offices and stopped before an old and battered-looking wagonette break, which had clearly had a hard life. The horse that was hitched in front matched the break in its tired demeanour. Richard followed his suitcase that had been lifted into the rear of the break and made himself comfortable as the man climbed up onto his seat and took up the reins.

'My name is Donald and the horse is called Sam,' the driver stated. 'Now hold on, sir, because Sam is sometimes too keen to get going.'

Donald shook the reins and made a loud cluck in his mouth in order to get Sam on the move. Sam flicked his ears but otherwise made no motion whatsoever.

'Move, ya dozy animal!' barked Donald, waving his whip, at which Sam took off like a greyhound after a hare. Unfortunately the weight of the break immediately slowed Sam's ambitious advance and he gave a grunt and a whinny, as if he had suddenly remembered that his days as a racehorse were finished and he was now destined to be a carthorse. It was good that Richard had followed Donald's advice to hold on, otherwise he could easily have ended up on his back on the road in front of the station ticket office.

Sam eventually settled into a steady pull and they progressed onto the new Nith Bridge. The grand stone structure of the Afton Hotel stood on the southern side of the road by the station, just before the start of the bridge. It had an extensive glazed porch and a set of wide steps leading down to the road. Apart from a maid, who paused in her cleaning of the windows to watch Richard pass, there did not seem to be anyone around the hotel.

As they crossed the bridge Richard looked down upon the river that he had viewed many times when the train from his home in Dumfries had sped him on his journey to his medical studies in Edinburgh. He had seen the river during its changing moods, from a lazy wander in the August heat to a marauding torrent in the winter months, when it burst over its banks to spread out over the meadows where cows had grazed during the warm summer days. A number of rounded hills were arranged on either side of its valley, like brooding elderly relatives awaiting their chance to voice disapproval.

Richard could see the bushes and reeds that marked the line of the River Afton, which joined the Nith not far downstream from the bridge. It brought to mind the poetry of Rabbie Burns, who had described this tributary as 'the sweet Afton'. He wondered what delights lay upstream that had filled the young Burns with such poetry. But as the shooting break passed over the end of the bridge he was assailed with the smell of the rubbish that had been thrown onto the river meadows, and of smoke from a smithy on the edge of the town.

'You'll be new in toon, sir,' Donald said from the front of the break. 'I don't remember seeing you here afore.'

'You're right,' replied Richard. 'I hae passed along the railway line many times, but this is my first time in New Cumnock toon itself.'

'Are you staying awhile then, sir?' asked Donald, 'Will ya be needing anywhere to stay?' Before Richard could answer his questions, he spoke again. 'It's just that my sister runs a braw boarding house in toon and I could get you a fair rate.'

'I believe that Dr Cluny may have made some arrangements for me to stay somewhere. I will need to wait until I have spoken to him.'

'This is the castle over there,' Donald explained, as if their discussion of accommodation had not taken place. 'William Wallace stayed there, when he was beating the English.' He pointed his whip towards the line of houses on the right, which formed a terrace alongside the road that was now beginning to rise up a slope. 'Not that you can see anything now. It's just a mound and some ditches. But it's still our castle,' he continued, with a touch of pride in his voice. 'We call this part of toon Castle.'

'You're a local man, then?' asked Richard.

'Och aye. Born and bred in this toon, just like my faither and his faither,' replied Donald.

The road was now bordered by houses on both sides. Many were shops, with large windows displaying a variety of goods. Some pots and pans hung outside an ironmonger's shop, and shovels, buckets, mops and other household items were stacked along the pavement below the window. Women, many in pairs and some with small children, walked purposefully along the pavements, whilst old men in large flat caps sat watching the street business. Donald acknowledged a pair of these old men, who were seated on some barrels, with a touch of his cap.

'This is the Castle Hotel,' said Donald, pointing to a large building set back slightly from the road. Two young men were leaning against a hitching rail, expectantly observing the approach of the break, perhaps hoping that Donald was bringing a new customer for the hotel. 'And across the way is the post office.'

As they continued further along the road it became clear to Richard that Castle, as Donald called it, was the main part of the settlement of New Cumnock, for as he passed the hotel the houses thinned out and on the right, alongside the hotel, there was a group of large trees whose branches overhung the road. As they passed them Richard could see a

grand house set back beyond the trees. Further down the road rose the square tower of the town church. The main body of the church had thin round castellated towers at each corner, with a pair of large arched Gothic windows on either side of the main door. The tower itself was topped with four pinnacles at each corner and a castellated wall between the pinnacles. Large Gothic and slatted windows, which presumably allowed the sound of ringing bells to alert the parishioners, were set into each face of the tower. It was an impressive church, set as it was, on its own, partway between Castle and another settlement that Richard could see further down the road. The church reminded Richard of pictures he had seen of corseted and stiff Georgian ladies with voluminous skirts.

Beyond the church were two more buildings, one of which was the Crown Inn. Donald didn't make any reference to these establishments but continued to follow the road until it turned sharply to the left by an ancient-looking building that dominated the roadside.

'This is the Old Mill,' said Donald, deciding to add to his commentary of New Cumnock. 'And this is the bridge over the Afton.' He pointed his whip towards a narrow stone bridge in the road ahead.

Richard craned his neck to look beyond the bridge, where he could see more houses and cottages spread out on either side. But just as Richard was anticipating looking over the parapet of the bridge at the river that Rabbie Burns had immortalised in his poem 'Sweet Afton', Donald pulled up Sam and the break drew to a halt.

Richard looked at the house in front of which they had stopped. It was a newly built two-storey stone house, which was unusual in the town, as most were either single-storey or cottages. This house also had dormer windows in the roof, so it had three floors and clearly had a lot of rooms. The front of the building was set back from the road, giving some room for a small front garden, which had become very fashionable in England.

'Here ye are then, young sir,' stated Donald, as he folded down the step to help Richard climb down from the back of the break. Once Richard was on the road, Donald leaned across to take the suitcase and bag, which he carefully deposited by the low wall at the front of the doctor's surgery.

'That'll just be tuppence,' Donald told Richard, holding out his hand.

Richard dropped two pennies in his hand.

'I'll be thanking ye,' responded Donald. 'Now, if ye need a bed tonight my sister's hoose is just a little further down the road, on the right. Just ask for Jeanie McClure.'

Richard thanked him, then collected his suitcase and bag and walked up the path to the front door of the house.

The door opened into a wide tiled hallway, with two rooms leading off on either side. A staircase led upstairs from one side of the hallway, and at its base, almost blocking the stairs, was a large leafy plant growing from a garish pot. Richard turned to his right, where he could hear voices, and saw a middle-aged woman with thick grey hair plaited behind her head. She looked up from the desk, behind which was clearly her domain.

'Can I help you, young man?' she asked severely.

'My name is Richard Robertson, Dr Richard Robertson. I am here to meet with Dr Cluny,' Richard nervously explained.

A smile broke out on the face of the woman as she quickly stood up and walked around the desk into the hallway. 'Dr Robertson, of course.

We have been expecting you. My name is Mrs Carr, Dr Cluny's secretary.' She offered her hand to Richard. He went to shake her hand but realised that he was still holding his suitcase, which he quickly put on the floor so that he could complete his greeting.

'Let me put your suitcase over here, whilst I inform Dr Cluny that you have arrived,' Mrs Carr continued, as she placed the suitcase alongside the large plant. 'Why don't you take a seat in the waiting room?'

She directed him into the waiting room, where wooden benches were placed along the walls. One old man was sitting on a bench, leaning slightly forward, holding a large cream-coloured handkerchief in front of him, as if he were about to sneeze or vomit. He looked up at Richard momentarily, before resuming his forward stare. He was the only occupant of the waiting room. The room was sparsely decorated with some pictures of rural scenes hanging on two walls.

'I'll just go and tell Dr Cluny,' Mrs Carr said, as she strode out of the waiting room and across the hallway.

Richard heard a conversation taking place just out of earshot, followed by a more audible man's voice saying, 'Tell him to come in.'

Mrs Carr reappeared. 'Dr Cluny will see you now, Dr Robertson.'

Richard walked through the door that Mrs Carr was holding open for him. It was clear that this was an examination room. A man in his late fifties, with a balding head and spectacles perched on his nose, was studying him from the middle of the room. Seated on a chair next to him was a young woman of about Richard's age, in her early twenties. She was looking at him curiously.

'I'm sorry, Dr Cluny, I didn't mean to disturb your examination,' Richard stuttered, stopping his walk into the room.

'No, that's fine, Dr Robertson, you come in. You have obviously worked out that I am Dr Cluny. Welcome.' He offered his hand, which Richard took. 'I might as well see if you are as good as Dr Watson at Edinburgh seems to believe. Join me for this examination and let's see what you make of this young lady's condition,' he continued, waving his arm at the young woman who had made Richard stop in his tracks. 'Now then, may I introduce Dr Robertson to you, Margaret? Dr Robertson, this is Margaret Craig.'

'Good afternoon, Mrs Craig,' Richard offered.

'Miss Craig,' Margaret corrected Richard, with a smile and with an emphasis on the *Miss*.

'Margaret has been troubled by a painful knee, so I would be interested in your diagnosis and suggested treatment.'

Richard got down on one knee, then looked up at Margaret's face. 'Could you let me have a look at both knees, please, so that I can compare them?'

'Of course, doctor,' she replied with a flirtatious smile, as she slowly pulled her skirt up her lower legs, revealing a pair of smooth white limbs.

Richard could not help but feel uncomfortable being in such intimate closeness to a young lady's legs. He deliberately avoided looking at Margaret and concentrated his attention on her knees. One knee was clearly red and swollen at the front.

'I assume that this is painful to touch, but how much movement do you have in it?' he asked Margaret.

'It is most painful when I try to kneel, but any movement will make it sore,' she explained.

Richard carefully touched the swollen area with his thumb, at which Margaret winced.

'I am sorry, Miss Craig, I am just trying to see if the area in front of the kneecap is soft or hard.'

'That's fine, doctor, you touch it as much as you want,' Margaret said softly and provocatively.

Richard found himself blushing and he turned to Dr Cluny. 'I believe that Miss Craig has a case of prepatellar bursitis. I would recommend that Miss Craig rest her knee and avoid kneeling until the swelling has diminished. If possible she should wrap the knee in a wet cloth to help reduce the swelling.'

'Very good, Dr Robertson.' Dr Cluny turned to Margaret Craig. 'You got a case of housemaid's knee, Margaret. You are going to have to tell your mother that she will have to find you other jobs around the house than scrubbing the floors.' He chuckled.

'It's being down on my knees looking after my cousin's wains that the problem. I seem to spend most of the day on the cold tiles,' Margaret explained.

'Well, you are going to have to get your sister to help out more with the wains, because your knee will not get better without some rest.'

Margaret pulled her skirts back over her legs and looked up at Richard, who was now standing next to her chair. 'So, doctor, are you going to be working here with Dr Cluny?' she enquired.

Before Richard could reply, Dr Cluny responded, 'Aye, we will give him a trial and see how he gets on. We need more help now that my son has opened his practice in Ayr.' He paused and looked expectantly at Richard. 'That's if you are willing to take the position, Dr Robertson.'

'I would be delighted, Dr Cluny,' Richard replied, moving forwards to shake Dr Cluny's hand again.

'Now, you take care of that knee, Margaret,' Dr Cluny said in a stern but friendly voice. 'I remember when you were wee, you were forever getting into scrapes and never listened to advice.'

'I am nearly an auld maid now, Dr Cluny; I'm no going to be climbing any more trees,' Margaret laughed as she limped from the examination room.

'I'll see your mither and faither at kirk on Sunday, so I'll remind them of our advice,' Dr Cluny said to Margaret's retreating back. He turned to Richard. 'Right, young man, we will need to get you sorted. I have arranged for you to stay with Mrs Johnstone, who has a spare room and is happy to have you lodge for a while. She is a widow and a formidable woman, but her bark is worse than her bite, as they say.' He chuckled at his own remark. 'Now, Mrs Carr will show the way, as I have one more patient to see. I will see you tomorrow morning and we will go through the paperwork.'

Richard left Dr Cluny to his examination and paused in the hallway, looking around at the surroundings with greater interest now that he realised that this house would be his new workplace. Mrs Carr welcomed him to the practice and told him that Dr Cluny would be glad of his assistance; the number of patients was increasing rapidly as more people had moved into the area with the new mines opening. She led him back to the road and gave him directions to Mrs Johnstone's house, back along the road in Castle.

Richard walked back along the road that he had travelled down in the break with Donald. He passed the Crown Inn, and as he was walking past the church he noticed a small group of three young women who were looking across at him. He recognised Margaret Craig as one of the group. The three all nodded to him, to which Richard smiled and returned their greeting. The three then turned away giggling as one of the women spoke in a quiet voice to the others. Richard felt himself blush slightly. He had grown up in an all-male household and had spent the last seven years in the all-male university in Edinburgh. The ways of women were a mystery to him.

He found the house where he was due to lodge and rapped on the door. It was a single-storey semi-detached house with dormer windows in the slate roof. The front doors of each property were side by side in the middle of the building and a low fence separated the small front gardens.

As Richard was studying the house and its surroundings the door suddenly swung open to reveal a middle-aged woman in a cotton dress that was tied tightly around her waist, emphasising her large bosom. Her hair was tied back into a bun. As Dr Cluny had described, she looked quite a fearsome woman.

'Good afternoon. My name is Dr Robertson, Richard Robertson. I believe that Dr Cluny has spoken to you about me lodging with you for a while,' Richard explained.

'Aye, Dr Robertson, Dr Cluny told me that you might be arriving today,' Mrs Johnstone replied. 'Come on in and I will show you the room.'

Richard followed her into the hallway and put his suitcase and bag to one side. He followed Mrs Johnstone into a room at the rear of the house. There was a single bed, a table with a wash basin and jug, a wardrobe and a small chest of drawers. The floor was stained brown and had polished wooden boards that still looked new, suggesting that this was a fairly new house. The window looked out onto a small back yard with fields beyond. It was a pleasant room.

'This looks fine, Mrs Johnstone. It will suit me very well.'

'That's good. Now, I have some rules. I don't want drink in the house; it is an abomination. If you smoke, then you do so out in the yard, not in the house.' She paused as other restrictions came into her mind. 'And, of course, you don't bring *women* back to the house,' she added, with a certain amount of disdain on the word *women*.

'That won't be a problem, Mrs Johnstone,' Richard replied.

Mrs Johnstone showed Richard around the rest of the house, including the outside toilet, of which she seemed very proud. After the tour Richard took his suitcase into his room and sat on the bed, staring out across the fields towards the distant hills. He thought back to the various turns he had taken, and the extraordinary fortune which had brought him to this exciting stage in his life. He could now, at last, carry out the profession for which he had been studying for the past ten years and more. He lay back on the bed and looked at the ceiling and smiled.

CHAPTER TWO

May 1869

It was the charming month of May,
When all the flowers were fresh and gay.
'The Charming Month of May', Robert Burns

It was the end of a warm spring day. The sun was setting, but it had left its warmth in the air and on the ground, helping the grass and hedgerows burst back into life. There was a flush of new life in the Nith valley. The trees wore their new green foliage, and groups of lambs had grown the courage to leave their mothers and race around the clumps of rushes dotted across the hillside.

John Baird had taken his milk cows down to the pastures close to the River Nith. It was early in the season to put them onto the flood meadows, but it had been a warm and dry February and there was grass there to feed his Ayrshire herd. He walked slowly back up the slope away from the railway line that now divided the main farm from the river meadows. He had often looked down the Nith valley and wondered who had decided to scar such a beautiful valley by putting such an unsightly construction down its length. He could still smell the soot from the train that had passed along the line just ten minutes previously. However, he knew that he shouldn't really complain; after all, he had just secured a contract to supply milk to the dairy in Glasgow, and the only way to get the milk to the dairy whilst still fresh was to use the railway.

John had taken up a lease on Meikle Garclaugh Farm, just outside New Cumnock, on the Mansfield estate. He considered this a good lease, as the laird, Sir James Stuart Menteath, was well known for the innovative improvement of agriculture on his farms. John had discussed the lease with the estate manager, or the factor, who had made it very clear that Sir James expected John to work hard and intelligently to improve Meikle Garclaugh. Sir James had an estate of nearly three thousand acres, which included coal mines and lime quarries, as well as arable land and pasture land in the estate farms. Although he was a man of considerable wealth he continued to seek improvements and had undertaken his own research into agricultural methods. He had even published a book on geology and had been instrumental in introducing the regular liming of land, despite the reluctance and occasional opposition of his tenants.

Nearing the collection of farm buildings that made up the steading, John could hear his new young wife Flora singing in the orchard as she collected in the washing. He smiled to himself and quickened his pace, hoping to surprise her. As he came alongside the trees that lined the orchard he could see Flora with her back to him, so he carefully squeezed through the trees and stepped over the fence.

Stealthily pacing across the grass, he came up behind her and wrapped his arms around her waist. Her quiet singing abruptly changed to a loud shriek, as she leapt in alarm and pushed him away. John roared with laughter and Flora grabbed his flat cap and began to batter him gently on the head. 'You daft rogue!' she said through her laughter. 'I nearly dropped the washing.' She grasped at her chest. 'My heart is pounding like one of those steam engines! Go on with you, John, you smell like one of your coos,' she exclaimed, pushing him away from her.

Chuckling at his own joke, John continued his walk up the orchard towards the house and the byre, where he planned to check on the Ayrshire bull that had recently been brought from his father's farm in Sorn, twenty miles to the north of New Cumnock. The Bairds of Blairkip were well known for breeding fine Ayrshire cattle and John was keen to expand the family's reputation down here in the Nith valley. As a tenant farmer he was never going to make a fortune from their farming skills and hard work, but, as his father used to say to his sons, 'Judge a man by his deeds, not by his money.'

John walked alongside the byre and then turned into the open yard formed by the buildings of the steading. His farm worker, James McCleon, was brushing down one of the plough horses outside the stable.

'You treat that horse better than some men treat their wives,' John greeted James.

'Well, she behaves better and works harder than many men's wives,' James replied, with a smile. James had worked on a number of farms and he knew some good farmers and some good men. He judged John Baird to be both.

John walked across to the Clydesdale horse and ran his hand across its back. The horse shivered at his touch, sending flies up into the air. He had three horses on the farm: two plough horses and one smaller one for the cart that took the milk to the station and Flora to the shops.

'Well, she's going to have to earn her keep soon. I have had a walk across the bottom fields and they are drying up very well,' said John. 'I want to get the barley sown, so I want you to harrow the top end tomorrow to get it ready for sowing next week. Let's hope that this good weather continues.'

'All right, boss. I will get the harrow ready before I go home,' James replied.

John patted the horse's withers and walked over to the end of one of the buildings that formed the north side of the steading square. The top part of a stable door stood open, and John leaned inside and peered into the dark interior. As his eyes became accustomed to the darkness he saw the shape of his new Ayrshire bull. It was busy chewing at some hay and it turned its head to look nonchalantly at him. The bull was a mix of white and brown patches, with its head and shoulders a darker brown, typical of the Ayrshire breed. It had been polled, by having its horns removed when it was young and then a hot iron put onto the stump to prevent regrowth of the horns. This made bulls much easier and safer to handle. To help lead it it also had a brass ring through its nose. This was done when the bull was still young, and then, to train it, the young bull was frequently led using a rope or a wooden pole with a clip at one end that fixed into the nose-ring. John had high hopes for his bull. If it proved to produce good offspring, he could rent it out to other farmers or even sell the young bulls it sired.

The day was drawing to a close, so John walked across the yard towards the dairy, which was next to the farmhouse. He kicked his boots against the wall of the barn to dislodge the mud that had stuck to the bottom and sides. At one end of the barn was the dairy itself, where the milk was stored and the cheeses were made. The dairy and the milking byre formed the west side of the steading and were painted with whitewash, as were all the walls. He could hear Maggie the dairy maid banging buckets and generally cleaning up after the afternoon's milking session.

The dairy was kept cool by allowing the wind to blow through slatted windows. The floor was made from large slabs of limestone, which were worn smooth by the boots of previous farmers and dairy maids. They were still wet from Maggie McCillan's cleaning regime.

John stood by the door and did not attempt to enter the spotless dairy. Despite being the boss, he dared not make Maggie angry by walking with his dirty boots on her clean floor. He had only done that once before and quickly regretted his mistake. John thoroughly respected Maggie, who was a skilled dairy worker and knew her business. Her Dunlop cheeses were sought after by local cheese merchants and helped to raise the reputation of the farm, as well as to bring in a regular income.

'Are you nearly done, Maggie?' he shouted through the dairy.

'Aye. Nearly done, Mr Baird,' replied Maggie. 'I just have to take the pans out of the steamer.'

The steamer was something that John had constructed to help sterilise the various pans and ladles used for processing the milk into cheese and cream. John had been taught about the importance of cleaning these implements, in order to kill off the germs that would make the milk go bad and spoil the cheeses. Not being able to afford to buy one of the new manufactured steamers, John had built one using an old water drum and pipes that he had got from the blacksmith. He was very proud of his homemade steamer that had cost a fraction of the cost of a factory-made one. Maggie had initially been dubious about this contraption, but once it was up and working she was satisfied that it did its job well and easily.

'I'll leave you to it, then, Maggie.'

John appreciated how fortunate he had been to hire Maggie as his dairy maid. She had been in high demand from other local farms and John could not easily compete with the wages that some would offer. Fortunately Flora, his wife, had been with him when he had spoken to Maggie at the May Fair in the previous year, and it was Flora who had led the negotiations and secured her services for a year. Flora and Maggie had formed an instant friendship, probably because they were the same age but also because they talked the same no-nonsense language. John often heard the two of them deep in conversation, usually followed by a hoot of shared laughter.

He turned and took the few steps to the back door of the house. He opened the door and entered the back place, where boots, coats and bits of farming equipment were either hanging or piled along the sides of the room. There was a glazed window at the far end, through which John could see that the daylight was fading fast.

Having removed his outer clothes, John stepped up onto the flagstones in the kitchen. He felt the heat from the range and smelt food being cooked. His stomach rumbled in anticipation.

Flora walked into the kitchen and, spotting him, gave a stern look. 'Now, keep your fingers out of the dinner, John Baird. I'll not having you fishing out the best bits afore they're ready.'

John threw his hands up in surrender. 'The thought ne'er crossed my mind, my dear. I would not risk another crack across my knuckles with yer ladle.'

He walked along the passageway that led past the stairs and into the room that served as his office. The room was dark, so he returned to the kitchen with the paraffin lamp, which he lit using a taper from the grate.

'I'll be glad when the summer days return and we can enjoy long evenings without lamps. It has been a long winter,' Flora said to John, as he was leaving the kitchen.

He paused in the doorway and looked upwards as he strained to recall a verse of poetry.

'*The flowery spring leads sunny summer*,' he finally remembered.

'My goodness, John, now you are quoting Rabbie Burns at me! Spring must be here!' They both laughed.

John took the lamp through to the office, but instead of settling down to do his paperwork, he left and went through to the parlour, where he walked to the window that looked out across the orchard and towards the Nith valley. In the distance he could see the outline of Dalhanna Hill as the last of the evening's light faded. John stood for a moment enjoying the beauty of the view, before quietly thanking God for bringing him to this place with the young wife that he loved.

CHAPTER THREE
June 1869

Upon a simmer Sunday morn,
When Nature's face is fair,
I walked forth to view the corn,
An' snuff the caller air.

'The Holy Fair', Robert Burns

The church had been nearly full for the Sunday service. Nowadays the Reverend Robert Murray always brought in a good congregation, but this had not always been the case. When he had first arrived, twenty-six years earlier, as minister at the Martyrs' Church of Scotland parish church, or the 'toon kirk', as most New Cumnock residents referred to it, he had been treated warily by the locals. He was now well respected and well liked and was a symbol of continuity in a town that was changing rapidly in so many ways. Now the congregation were filing out of the kirk and Reverend Murray was standing by the doors, exchanging words with everyone as they left. It was a beautiful summer's day and sun was warming the members of the congregation.

Richard was standing just behind the main doors, awaiting his turn to leave the kirk. In front of him were a couple, the man dressed in a woollen suit. The man was in his late thirties and looked very uncomfortable in his suit. He kept putting his fingers behind his collar to try to find more room for his neck.

'Stop fiddling with your collar, John; you'll make it grubby and it will be a bother to clean,' Richard heard the lady say to her husband.

'I'm just glad that I only have to squeeze into this outfit once a week. In this heat I will have lost a bucket of sweat by the time we get home,' was the muttered reply.

The couple stepped forward to be greeted by Reverend Murray.

'Good day to you, John and Flora. How are you both?'

John shook Reverend Murray's hand vigorously, clearly keen to speed up the greeting. 'We are both fine, thank you, Reverend Murray, just like the weather.'

'Aye, the good Lord has blessed us today.' Reverend Murray looked behind John and Flora, so John made to walk away. But Reverend Murray caught his arm to stop him.

'Now, John, have you met our new doctor in toon, Richard Robertson?'

Richard started at the mention of his name and looked up at Reverend Murray.

'Richard, can I introduce you to Mr and Mrs Baird, who farm at Meikle Garclaugh over the river?' Reverend Murray asked. 'Richard has been working with Dr Cluny since April, and word in the toon is that he is making a good impression. He has become a member of our congregation; I am surprised that you haven't met yet. Can I leave you to introduce yourselves?'

Reverend Murray then moved on to greet other members of his congregation, leaving Richard, John and Flora to shake hands.

'So where do you call hame, Dr Robertson?'

'I was born and grew up in Dumfries, Mrs Baird,' Richard replied courteously, feeling a little as if he were being inspected.

'Just call us Flora and John,' laughed Flora, making the atmosphere seem much less formal.

'And please call me Richard. I get called Dr Robertson too much as it is.'

'Well, that tends to go with the profession,' John responded.

The three turned and walked away from the church doors and towards the road. Flora touched Richard gently on the arm and spoke quietly to him. 'When Reverend Murray says that you have made a good impression, Richard, he may be referring to the impression that you have made on some of the young women in toon. I have heard our maid talking about this handsome young bachelor doctor who has come to toon.'

Richard blushed and threw a smile at Flora. He tried to mutter a response, but nothing seemed appropriate. At twenty-five Flora was about the same age as him, and she had a kindly but piercing gaze. She was striking in many ways and was clearly a woman who had her own opinions. John was a stocky man with a bushy beard under his chin. His eyes were equally piercing and overhung by bushy eyebrows. Richard could perceive a fine mind behind his eyes, which twinkled with a mischievous spirit. Despite being in their company for such a short time, he found himself warming to them.

'Stop teasing the man, Flora,' laughed John. 'I am sure that he gets enough pestering from all the eligible women as it is.'

'So where are you staying just now, Richard?' asked Flora.

'I have a room with Mrs Johnstone.' He paused. 'It does me just fine and has a lovely view up the valley towards the lochs.'

'Let's hope the view stays fine, because there is lots of talk of sinking mines over that way,' John said. 'Well, it's been nice to meet you, Dr Robertson. If you ever get over towards Mansfield, you must call by and I will show you Meikle Garclaugh.'

'Wheesht, John! Not everyone is interested in looking at your coos,' Flora teased her husband.

'I live in a farming area, Flora,' Richard said. 'I need to learn about my patients' way of life, as it will help me to understand their illnesses. I would love to visit you both at your farm.'

'Well, why don't ye come over for lunch one Sunday? I am sure that you could do with a break from Mrs Johnstone's cooking. That'll be all right, won't it, John?' It was a more of a challenge to John than a question.

'That would be grand, Richard. It will give me a break from having to listen to Flora and our dairy maid, Maggie, blethering about some handsome young doctor in toon,' responded John with a hearty laugh.

'I will happily accept your invitation,' replied Richard.

They all shook hands and Richard stood for a while watching John and Flora walk up the road towards a tethered horse and carriage. He had met many people since his arrival in town and had had many invitations for meals. He had enjoyed most of these invitations, but many had clearly been arranged for him by families who were seeking a good husband for their daughter. He was far too busy in his new position to concern himself with matrimony. Besides, none of the women who had been preened and paraded in front of him attracted him at all. None, except the first young woman he had met on the day of his arrival. He had since met Margaret Craig on a number of occasions around the town. They always exchanged pleasant conversation and Margaret usually made him smile with an amusing remark. She was friendly and did not push herself on him like so many of the other young women. In quiet moments during the day he had found himself thinking about her.

However, on this glorious summer's day Richard had decided that he would walk up the Afton valley and explore the river that had brought poetry out in Rabbie Burns. He shook himself out of his thoughts and strode purposefully towards his lodgings. Mrs Johnstone had offered to make him up a lunch and a flask of water for his walk. He had also bought some strong breeches for the walk, and Dr Cluny had lent him his good hickory walking stick. There would be no problem with the route; it was just a case of following the River Afton upstream.

Once he had changed and collected the lunch that Mrs Johnstone had left for him on his table, he set off down the road towards Afton Bridgend. Here the road split, with one branch going east towards Kirkconnel, whilst the other road headed south west. This latter road led past the industrial area of New Cumnock, where iron furnaces and coal pits belched their black smoke into the air. Richard mused that Rabbie Burns would have breathed in air unpolluted and untainted with the smell of soot.

However, on reaching the junction next to the Old Mill, Richard took neither road but a footpath that went behind the school and met the banks of the Afton just below the bridge. The footpath followed the river and Richard strode on, using the walking stick to knock back the long grasses and the brambles that stretched their tendrils across the path in search of new ground to colonise. Bramble blossom was forming that would later become the delicious blackberries, the only grace of these voracious, prickly weeds whose tough tendrils could easily trip an unwary walker.

After a short distance Richard's path met the mill stream that came off the Afton and took water down to the pond behind the corn mill at the road junction. It was only a narrow stream, so he was able to leap across it with little effort. He then cut across a meadow by the river where some cattle were grazing on the spring pasture. They took little interest in him, only moving slightly out of his way to find new grass. Across the river he could see West Park farm and he soon came across the ford that allowed carts to cross the river, taking goods and passengers to the farmhouse.

As Richard continued his walk the banks became steeper and it was harder to walk alongside the river. He scrambled up a bank through the trees to the roadway that went up the valley. Here it was much easier to walk, although he was further from the river that he was intent on following. Eventually he came to a track that seemed to lead down to the river. He followed it and came to another ford, where there were stepping stones that allowed walkers to cross the river with dry feet.

He came across a young couple lying in the grass beside the track. They were clearly courting and jumped up at the sound of Richard's approach, the girl looking very sheepish as she smoothed her shirts and brushed off the grass.

Richard greeted them, hoping to make them feel less conscious of their discovery.

'Good afternoon. Can you tell me where this track leads?' he asked, pointing his stick along the track that led up from the ford.

'Aye, sir,' the lad replied. 'It leads up to Over Dalhanna farm.'

'I'm following the river up Glen Afton,' Richard explained. 'Is this path an easy route?' He gestured to a path that seemed to lead along the side of the river.

'Aye, sir, that's a guid path that will tak ye right up the glen.'

Richard gave his thanks and turned away to take the path that the lad had shown him. The girl could barely have been sixteen and he wondered if her mother knew what her daughter was getting up to on a Sunday morning.

The path took him across another meadow before rejoining the river. He decided to find himself somewhere to sit and have his packed lunch. As he approached the river he heard voices and then laughter. Someone else had also decided to have their lunch by the river. He did not want to disturb them, so he looked for another path.

He saw that the meadow headed towards some trees, so he left the footpath and walked towards the trees. There was a fence where the meadow ended and he saw that he could climb over and walk alongside the river. As he lifted himself over the fence, the leg of his trousers caught on one of the upright sticks. His momentum was taking him forwards, but his leg was left firmly attached to the fence. Eventually the stick broke and he tumbled down the bank into the river. Fortunately the river was shallow and, apart from some wet clothes, he was unharmed. He looked around to rescue the bag with his lunch and retrieve the walking stick that had proved to be very ineffective at preventing his fall down the bank.

'Good afternoon, Dr Robertson,' a voice announced itself. 'It's a lovely warm day to take a dip in the river.'

Richard looked up to see Margaret Craig standing beyond the fence. She was smiling down at him.

'Are you unharmed, doctor, or do we need to administer some medical attention to you?'

'I am fine, Miss Craig, if somewhat wet and embarrassed,' Richard replied.

'So what made you want to leave the path which gives travellers such a sound footing?'

'I was taking a wee detour in order to avoid disturbing your lunch. An intention that I clearly failed to achieve.' By now Richard had scrambled back up the bank to stand in front of Margaret. She wore a light-coloured cotton dress and the sun shone through it, producing a silhouette of her slim figure. He paused as he became aware of this erotic image in front of him. Margaret was also aware of his observation and smiled to herself.

'Why don't you come over and join us? It's just my faither, mither and my wee sister Lizzie. We are quite harmless, I promise.'

Margaret's blue eyes and radiant smile instantly distracted him from his expedition and he gratefully accepted the invitation.

Richard had met Margaret's mother and younger sister previously, when they had been in the surgery visiting Dr Cluny. He was introduced to Margaret's father, who was the manager at the City of Glasgow Bank in Pathhead, on the other side of the Nith Bridge. Richard settled down to enjoy his lunch along with the Craig family. The conversation flowed easily and Richard realised how much he was missing his own family. He vowed to find time to return to Dumfries and visit.

After lunch had been eaten, Mr Craig took Elizabeth off to look for butterflies, which were a particular interest for him. Mrs Craig was busy packing away the remains of their meal. She turned to Margaret.

'Why don't you show Dr Robertson the safe way up to the footbridge? His trousers have nearly dried in the sun, although his boots are going to be wet for a while longer.'

Margaret looked expectantly at Richard, who smiled and climbed to his feet. He collected his bag and stick and they set off along the footpath, which took them around the trees and across a meadow. They talked easily and Richard found himself enjoying her company. She was intelligent and educated, as well as having a good sense of humour.

They soon reached the footbridge, where they paused to watch the River Afton bumbling over the pebbles as dragonflies flitted about the flowers that grew on both banks. Richard gazed at the scene and realised that he had found some of the delights that had inspired Rabbie Burns, including the company of an attractive young woman.

'You look like a man at ease, Dr Robertson,' Margaret said gently.

'Please call me Richard.'

'Only if you stop calling me Miss Craig and call me Margo.'

They both laughed and returned their gaze to the gentle River Afton.

'I was enjoying the scenery, as much as I have enjoyed your company, Margo,' Richard said after a while.

Margaret looked into his eyes and smiled. 'Well, I think it's best if you take me back to Burnfoot, Richard. My faither will be wanting us to start back for the toon. On these long summer days it is easy to lose track of the time.'

They crossed the river and joined the roadway back down to the junction in the river where they had had their lunch. The Craig family had packed up and were ready for the long walk back to New Cumnock. Richard joined them on the walk back, Mr Craig asking exploratory questions about Richard's past. Richard told them about his university life, but chose not to provide too much detail about his early life and his family.

The walk back to town was over far too quickly for Richard, who parted company with the Craig family outside his lodgings. He had never made it to the top of the glen to see the view, but had found a much more pleasant vision.

CHAPTER FOUR
July 1869

My father was a farmer upon the Carrick border,
And carefully he bred me in decency and order.
'My Father Was a Farmer', Robert Burns

After the church service some weeks later, Richard joined John and Flora Baird in their carriage back to their farm. It was another warm summer's day and Richard could not help but notice that John was glancing at the sky at various times with a concerned expression.

'Are you worried about rain, John?' he asked.

'Aye, the grass is cut and ready for turning. I don't want any rain to delay the hay making.'

'Wheesht, John! There's not a cloud in the sky,' remarked Flora. She turned to Richard. 'You'll find that oot about farmers, Richard. If they're not worrying about something, then they're not happy.'

After they had crossed the bridge over the river and then the railway, John turned the horse onto the Mansfield road, at the crossroad in Pathhead. The buildings on either side of the road were a mix of two-storey houses and the single-storey cottages that were characteristic of West Scotland. They had long windows on either side of a central door and were usually whitewashed with lime. The row of houses of different heights and different shades of white reminded Richard of the teeth of a patient that he had examined a few days previously.

They passed through the small settlement of Mansfield and then the road cut between fields that had opened up on either side. Straight ahead, in the distance, were hills spread out towards the large dome of Corsencon Hill to the south, looking like the torso and the bosom of a woman lying on her back. The fields to Richard's right looked lush and cows were grazing on the rich grass. On his left, however, the land wore coarse grasses interspersed with clumps of rushes, amongst which sheep and some beef cattle were searching for sweeter grass.

Richard leaned forward towards John. 'Why is there such a difference between the fields on either side of the track, John?'

'That's down to good management. The laird has always encouraged the use of lime on the fields, which improves the soil and the grass. He followed his faither's system and has been using lime on these fields for many, many years now, so you can see the difference it makes. He limed the fields on the right, but has not yet done those up the hill.' John pointed. 'The laird has a number of lime kilns on the estate, which he uses to sell the lime, as well as improve the land.'

'I have only ever seen him and his wife pass by in their carriage,' Richard noted. 'He must be an interesting person to meet.'

'I have only met him a couple of times,' John replied. 'Not long after I took on the tenancy he came over with the factor to meet me. He's an old man now, pushing eighty years old, but he still seems fairly fit and active.'

They had passed some cottages and in the distance Richard could see the buildings of farm steadings, both to his right and further up the slope of the hill to his left. Before he could ask, John began to identify the various groups of buildings.

'This is the Mains on the right. Jack Picken and his wife Jean have been farming there for over twenty years.' John then waved towards the further buildings to his left. 'That's Mansfield Hall over there. Will Gilmour and his wife Katherine run that place.'

The carriage approached a clump of trees, through which Richard could make out the outline of a large house.

'And this is Mansfield House, where the laird lives,' John said with emphasis. 'He has another estate down in Dumfriesshire called Closeburn, so he spends his time between the two houses. But it is this estate with its coal pits and lime kilns that really keeps his interest. It's also where his money comes from.'

As the carriage passed over a narrow bridge, traversing a small river that tumbled down the hillside, the drive to Mansfield House came into view on the right. Richard studied the building itself. It was not a pretty house, having clearly been extended with additional

Meikle Garclaugh Farm.

buildings over the years, giving it a jumbled appearance. The house seemed to be in three sections, which gradually got smaller to the east, with a Gothic arched entrance in the central, narrowest section. The slate roofs wore a crown of tall chimneys that would take the smoke from the coal fires up and over the trees that surrounded the site like a parade of guardsmen.

'And this is the land that I farm,' John explained proudly, pointing over the fields that sloped down towards the River Nith. 'And there is Meikle Garclaugh steading.' The house and farm buildings could now be seen positioned at the top of the slope, not far from the road.

'Is there a Wee Garclaugh, John?' Richard asked.

'Aye, there is a Wee Garclaugh. My neighbour James Houston and his wife Helen farm there. It's just a little further down this road.'

'And when did you take on this farm?'

'We moved in here three years ago,' John said. 'I grew up at Sorn. The Bairds have been farming up there for generations, so this was quite a move for us.'

'Is that where your family come from, Flora?' Richard asked.

'No, my family came from Auchinleck, near Old Cumnock. My faither has a farm called Back Rogerton. He farms it with my brothers James and William.'

'Enough with all yer questions now, Richard. Here we are.' John guided the horse off the main roadway and down the farm track towards the house and the steading. The layout of the steading was typical of most farms, with a square of buildings around a courtyard. The house, standing higher than the rest, formed the south side of the square. The house had two floors, but the slate roof came halfway down the second storey, so that three bedroom windows were partly in the wall and partly gabled out of the roof. This was a common feature in Ayrshire houses that had originally been single-storey cottages but had then had a second floor added.

John slowed the horse next to one of the farm buildings. Richard climbed out of the carriage and then helped Flora to descend.

'Thank you, Richard. I will just go indoors to see what mess the maid has made of our lunch,' she chuckled, as she hoisted her long skirts and tiptoed across the puddles that were dotted around the yard. John busied himself with the horse, unhitching it from the carriage and undoing the various leather straps that attached the horse to its harness.

Richard looked around the yard. There were two long low buildings, with slate roofs, that formed the west and the north sides of the square. They were whitewashed and there were three doors at various places along the walls. The smell of cows drifted across the yard and he could hear an animal coughing in one of the buildings.

Suddenly there was a commotion over by the house and Richard turned to see a girl of about fifteen years chasing two or three chickens out of one of the side doors. He could hear Flora's loud voice shouting orders and the girl stopped, glanced across at him and then quickly disappeared back into the house.

'Let me take you round to see the farm, Richard,' John said, as he guided Richard towards a doorway in the building behind him. 'This will take you through to the orchard, where we can see over the valley,' he explained.

John took Richard around to the garden area to the rear of the house. In front of him was spread the Nith valley, with New Cumnock over to his right. The fields sloped down towards a railway line and then they continued on to the river beyond it. On the other side of the valley rose the various hills that made up the bulk of the Knipe. It was a majestic panorama.

'That's quite a view that you have here, John.'

'Aye, it allows me to see any bad weather that's heading oor way, as well as keeping an eye on what's happening in the fields,' John replied nonchalantly. He turned to look at Richard. 'It helps to remind me of God's majesty as well.'

'It does that, John, it does that.'

'Now let's go inside and I will pour ye a wee dram.'

*

Richard, John and Flora had finished their meal of boiled chicken and vegetables. Flora had been up from the table several times to oversee the work of the maid in the kitchen. The maid had only been taken on at the recent hiring fair and she was still young and inexperienced, so Flora had to train her in housework and cooking. Richard heard her chastising the girl. 'Didn't yer mither teach you anything, girl? Now go through and clear the table, and take care.'

The girl appeared in the dining-room doorway looking flustered and hot. John looked up as she tiptoed towards the table, and he gave her a wink and a smile.

'Now take care with the china, Jessie, it's only the third time that we have used it since the wedding.'

'Aye, Mr Baird,' Jessie replied nervously. She carefully lifted a china bowl that had held the cooked green beans.

'So, Richard, was your faither also a doctor?' asked John.

'No, he was in farming,' replied Richard. This was the answer that he always gave to this question. He hoped that John would not probe any further.

'So you didn't follow him, then?'

'No, I was fortunate to have the opportunity to study medicine,' Richard replied briefly.

'You were indeed a fortunate man; not many farmers can afford to send their sons to university,' John said. 'So, do you have many brothers and sisters back in Dumfries?'

'I have three brothers.' But before John could continue with his questioning Richard responded with his own question. 'So, what about yourself, John? Do you come from a big family?'

'Aye, I have four brothers and three sisters. We grew up on a farm called Coplar, near Sorn. Then, when I was about thirteen, we moved over to this other neighbouring farm called South Blairkip. There was another farm across the fields called North Blairkip. Our cousins farm that place, so there were a guid number of Bairds in that area. Every second person you spoke to seemed to be a Baird. I had so many cousins and distant cousins that I never did work out how we were all related. My grandmither, Margaret Struthers, seemed to know how we were all connected, but when you are young you're not interested in listening to the auld folk, are you?'

John paused and waited for Richard to speak, but he did not seem inclined to share his own family information, so John continued. 'I can remember my grandmither telling me that my grandfaither, Thomas, was born on this estate. It was called Garrive in those days. A new laird came, Monteath's grandfaither it must have been, and changed the name to Mansfield, because that was his wife's name. At least that's what I have been told.'

Flora came back into the room. 'Now I hope he's not blethering on about his coos, Richard. It's his usual topic of conversation.'

Richard laughed. 'No, John was telling me that he has come back to his grandfaither's birthplace.'

'Well, we are not so sure if it was here that he was born, or on one of the other farms on the estate,' John explained.

'Now would you like to try some currants, Richard?' Flora asked. 'They are quite tart, but I've added a little bicarb and some sugar to take the edge off them.' She placed bowls of boiled redcurrants in front of Richard and her husband, in anticipation of a positive answer to her question.

'You are spoiling me, Flora. I haven't eaten so well for a long time,' Richard responded.

In the mid-afternoon John said that he would have to get changed in order to fetch the cows in for milking. Richard thanked John and Flora and told them that he would walk back to his lodgings.

'If you hang about for me to get changed I will walk with you down to the river and I'll show you the path that you can take to the bridge,' John suggested.

So John and Richard walked down the farm track towards the river. The sun was still high and house martens and swallows filled the sky, as they made the most of the bounty of insects driven up from the fields by the grazing cattle. As they approached the railway line Richard could see that the farm track went up the bank, across the railway lines and down the other side. However, the cows were grazing in the field on the far side of the railway embankment.

'Is it easy to get the cows over the railway line, John?' Richard asked.

'They do get rather skittish as we cross over. Fortunately we know the timetable for the trains, so we can make sure that we avoid them. Unfortunately they sometimes send down a goods train that is not on a regular timetable, so we have to keep our ears and eyes open. You see them long before you can hear them. Their smoke can be seen from a long distance down the valley. We haven't had any bother, but a farmer down the valley had a couple of his coos killed when they were crossing over.'

'Did they get any compensation?'

'Naw. The railway companies just say that the coos should not have been on the track,' John said. 'At this time of year we use the river meadows for hay, so we keep the coos off those fields. But once the hay has been collected we put them on to clear up what hay has not been picked up. Now then, Richard, if you cross the railway line and walk down to the river, you will see the path that runs alongside it. You have to cross a couple of burns on the way, but you will see where folk have put logs to help with the crossing. Have a safe walk home and thank you for your company.'

Richard returned the thanks and set off along the farm track. From the top of the railway embankment he could see the flat flood meadows in which the grass had been cut and was drying in the sun, slowing turning into hay. He disturbed some curlews, which glided across the lines of hay, calling out their mournful cries. As he walked across the meadow he could feel the ground bouncing under his steps, indicating the wet boggy soil that was characteristic of these meadows. As he got closer to the river bank he could make out the path of flattened grass.

He had expected to see a river as clear and picturesque as the Afton had been on the previous Sunday. Instead the river was grey and gave off a smell of sewage. He noticed that the river bank was sloped down at one point, where the cows had come down to drink. He was repelled at the thought of the cows drinking this polluted water. He wondered if it would affect the milk that they produced. Later, as he neared the point where the Afton joined the Nith, he could see that the sweet Afton was equally grey with effluent. The town was growing, so this problem would only get worse, thought Richard.

CHAPTER FIVE
February 1870

As well as the usual snow lying over the hills and filling the hollows with deep drifts, there was a cold wind from the north that made the people walking between the shops in Castle cover their faces with scarves and hurry to the warmth of the next shop. Richard paused outside the hotel to rub the forehead of a horse that was harnessed to a break. 'Hello, Sam,' he said quietly, and Sam responded to his gentle tone by turning his head to snort in his direction and seemingly rub his forehead on Richard's hand.

'He likes you, Dr Robertson,' a voice said behind Richard. Richard turned to see Donald standing in the doorway of the hotel. 'Are ye looking for a lift, sir?' Donald was always on the look-out for custom.

'No, thank you, Donald, not just now. But I will be sure to look for you if I am in need.'

He gave Sam a last pat and walked on along the icy pavement. As he was passing Kirkland's drapery shop he glanced through the window to see Flora Baird. He stepped into the shop, grateful to escape the icy wind and enter the warm embrace and homely smell of the drapery. Flora was busy examining some cloth, so he did not disturb her deliberations. He turned his attention to some woollen scarves that were on display.

'There are some more scarves in the store, Dr Robertson, if you don't see anything you like here,' a woman's voice said next to him. It was Mrs Kirkland, who managed the drapery part of the Kirkland business. Richard responded with his thanks and noticed that Flora was now making her way over to him.

'Good morning, Richard. I hope that you are well?' she enquired.

'I am well, thank you, Flora,' he replied.

'Och, a doctor would not be getting many patients if he didn't keep himself healthy!' Flora laughed.

'How are you keeping, Flora?' Flora was eight months pregnant and even her thick winter clothing didn't hide her large bump.

'I am doing very well, thank you, Richard, although this wee laddie seems to be wanting to arrive early, considering how much he is kicking.'

'You are certain that it is a boy, then?'

'Well, if it is a girl she will have some strong legs on her.' Flora winced as she felt another kick. They both laughed. 'That settles it; it is definitely a boy. Only a boy would get upset about being called a girl.'

'How's John?' Richard asked.

'Och, he's fine. Oor neighbour at the Mains, Jack Picken, has been trying to persuade John to join the curling team, so he plans to head up to Lochside this afternoon where the team is practising. They have a big competition for the Eglington Jug coming up soon.'

'I didn't realise John was a curler.'

'Aye, his kin up at Sorn are all keen curlers, so all the menfolk get drawn into it,' Flora said. 'You must remember, Richard, that for most of the rest of the year it is too busy on the farms to spare the time for games. They are very keen on curling in New Cumnock and they have a good team. Why don't you give it a try?'

'I will give it some thought. Perhaps it will help me to meet more of the community as well.'

Richard gave his farewell and left Flora to finish her shopping. As he continued his walk he spotted Margo Craig on the other side of the road. When he was about to cross the road he became aware of a carriage coming down the road at some speed from the direction of the hotel. He recognised it as belonging to Mansfield House. The coachman slowed the horses to come alongside him. The coachman leaned down towards Richard.

'Dr Robertson. They said at the surgery that you would be here at Castle. We have need of a physician at the house and Dr Cluny is not available. Your bag is in the carriage.'

Richard was very taken aback by the request, or was it an order? Whatever it was, he did not have the impression that it would be wise to refuse. As he climbed into the carriage the coachman set off quickly, throwing Richard into the seat. He glimpsed Maggie looking across at

Mansfield House.

him, as the street rushed past the window of the carriage, but did not even have time to give her a wave.

Richard was very grateful for the closed carriage which reduced the worst effects of the cold wind. The road to Mansfield House was a good road, unlike many of the roads in the area, which had become deeply rutted, making carriage journeys not only uncomfortable but dangerous. The carriage eventually drew up in front of the main door of Mansfield House and the coachman jumped off to help him descend.

The front door of the house opened and an anxious-looking woman in her mid-thirties stepped out. 'Thank you for coming, doctor. Sir James requires your attention.' She ushered him into the warm interior of the house.

The maid offered to take his overcoat. 'If you just wait here, doctor, I'll take you up to Sir James's room.'

The housemaid disappeared into a side room with his coat and Richard was left to examine the hall. To his right he could see a drawing room through the half-opened door. There were a couple of settees around a coal fire, along with small tables and the other furnishings of a room that is used for comfort. The hallway was lit by a window to his left and also by light through the door of another room further along the hall to his right. A corridor alongside the staircase disappeared into the dimly lit bowels of the house beyond.

On the walls were hung various paintings of family members, looked down upon by a row of deer antlers that were fixed to wooden plaques bearing inscriptions on small brass plates. No doubt these bore the dates of when and where these magnificent animals were shot, Richard thought. At the end of the row, looking like an intruder, was the stuffed head of some African antelope that Richard could not identify. A dark wood staircase, with a patterned carpet, led up the side of the wall.

The housemaid reappeared and motioned for Richard to follow her up the stairs. On each step there were highly polished brass rods held in place by brass fittings on either side of the carpet. These kept the carpet in place and prevented it from slipping away under the feet of the users. Halfway up the stairs the maid half-turned and said, as if some warning were required, 'Lady Jane is with Sir James.'

At the top of the stairs the maid led Richard to the right, along the landing to a room at the south of the house. She paused in front of a door and knocked quietly. A voice from beyond the door told her to enter.

The maid pushed open the door, paused in the doorway and curtsied. 'Dr Robertson is here, madam.' She looked expectantly at Richard and used her eyes to indicate that he was to enter the room.

The bedroom was quite dark as the windows still had the drapes over them. Some candles had been lit, which threw a flickering light over the large four-poster bed where Sir James was resting. He was wearing a nightgown and a cotton nightcap.

Next to the bed, sitting on a chair, was Lady Jane Stuart Menteath. She stood and took a step towards Richard to study him. 'You are young, Dr Robertson.'

Richard didn't know whether to agree with this statement or to defend himself against the accusation of inexperience that was implied. Before he could answer, she continued. 'However, I have heard good reports from Dr Cluny about you. Sir James's usual doctor is in Glasgow, but Dr Cluny steps in when an emergency arises. It seems that we have a bit of an emergency, Dr Robertson. Sir James had some kind of episode this morning as he was rising from his bed to dress. Once the fitting had stopped we managed to get him back into bed, but since then he has been still and we have been unable to wake him.'

Richard questioned Lady Jane about the circumstances of the episode and his previous health. He then examined Sir James thoroughly. He noted how one side of his face seemed to have relaxed more than the other. Richard had seen a similar case when he was training in Edinburgh. Eventually he returned his stethoscope to his bag and turned to Lady Jane.

'I believe that Sir James has suffered a stroke, which is caused by a bleed into his brain from a burst blood vessel. Sometimes the patient can recover, but often they are left with disabilities and are unable to speak or walk properly. There is nothing that I can do for him other than to advise that you continue to provide warmth and attempt to get him to drink water and eat some food. We must then wait to see if he wakes up and starts to recover. However, considering Sir James's age, this may take some time.'

Lady Jane looked at him with steely eyes as she absorbed everything that Richard had told her. She then looked at her husband in the bed for a short while before speaking.

'Thank you for your candour, Dr Robertson. From what I understand about strokes, even if my husband survives this episode, it is unlikely that he will be fit enough to run the estates for a considerable time.'

'I would agree with your assessment of the situation, Lady Menteath.'

'Very well. My husband's usual doctor is not able to arrive until tomorrow. What do you prescribe as a treatment in the meantime?'

'If you put some pillows behind him and keep him as upright as possible, this will reduce the blood flow to his brain. It is possible that he may fit again, so it is important that someone stays with him at all times to prevent him choking.'

'Is there no medicine or treatment that you can prescribe?'

'I'm afraid that there is no effective treatment for this condition. However, your husband's usual doctor may be able to suggest something. I am sure that he will have more experience of these types of afflictions than myself.' Richard packed up his bag and closed it. He stood for a while looking at the pale body of the old man struggling to hang on to life. Richard did not believe that Sir James had much time left in this world.

Lady Jane moved across to the wall, where she pulled on a woven rope hanging from a pulley near the ceiling. A few moments later the door opened and the housemaid appeared. Lady Jane turned to Richard. 'Janet will escort you back to the carriage. Thank you for coming so promptly, Dr Robertson.'

Richard could not work out whether her indifferent manner was hiding her real emotions or whether she really was as unconcerned as she appeared. He left the room, retrieved his overcoat and returned to the cold air outside. The coachman took Richard back to the surgery at a gentler pace than had brought him to Mansfield House.

About two hours later Dr Cluny returned from his trip to Ayr to learn of Richard's trip to Sir James's bedside. He listened carefully to Richard as he described Sir James's state and then to the advice that he had given to Lady Jane. He stood for a while with his chin propped in his cupped hand.

'Well, from what you have described of his condition it sounds as if you have made the correct diagnosis and he has had a stroke. At his age, he is unlikely to survive long. I know Dr Chapman from Glasgow. I am sure that he will support your diagnosis as well.' He paused and then looked at Richard. 'This may bring a lot of changes to the Mansfield estate.'

Richard looked at Dr Cluny in a puzzled manner.

'Sir James has no children,' Dr Cluny explained, 'and as far as I am aware his heir is his nephew, who is also called James. From what I have heard his nephew spends most of his time in New York, where he has business and many other interests. We will have to see if he decides to take an interest in the Closeburn and Mansfield estates that he is likely to inherit.'

Richard realised that this could have an impact on John and Flora, as well as the other tenant farmers around New Cumnock.

Dr Cluny continued. 'However, in the meantime, you must not speak of this to anybody. If he does make a recovery we do not want to be accused of spreading false rumours of his impending demise.'

'Of course, Thomas,' Richard replied. 'I always keep patient information confidential.'

Dr Cluny turned and placed a reassuring hand on his shoulder before disappearing into his room.

*

Two days later Richard was in his surgery when Mrs Carr knocked on the door and came in.

'Just to let you know, Richard, that it has been announced that Sir James Stuart Menteath passed away yesterday evening.'

'Thank you, Jane,' replied Richard.

'Dr Cluny will send a letter of condolence from the practice,' Jane Carr continued, as much to herself as to Richard. 'He was a good laird. Unlike some of the absent lairds, he always kept an interest in his estates and worked hard to improve them. He has been at Mansfield for nearly twenty-five years. We don't know much about the new laird. We will have to wait and see.' She closed the door, leaving Richard to ponder on the situation. Sir James's demise was unlikely to affect him very much, but it would bring some changes in the town.

CHAPTER SIX

March 1870

The snowdrop and primrose our woodlands adorn,
And violets bathe in the wet of the morn.

'My Nanie's Awa', Robert Burns

At Meikle Garclaugh, Flora was busy around the house, as always, when she heard Jessie, her maid, talking to someone in the kitchen. She left her tidying and walked through to find Helen Houston from Wee Garclaugh and her daughter. They were both warming their hands in front of the range, which was set in the wall of the kitchen beneath a large beam.

'Hello there, Flora. I hope ye dinna mind me callin' on yer. We've bin in a real pickle since we heard of the laird passing. We wondered if ye have heard anything about what is going on with the new laird.'

'Well, it's only been a few days, Helen. No one really knows what is happening. Why don't ye tak a seat and we'll warm some milk for yer both?' Flora turned to Helen's nine-year-old daughter, who was also called Helen. 'Now then, wee Helen, I've hidden away some tablet from Mr Baird, otherwise he wud eat it all. Wud ye like some?'

Helen, who had been staying close to her mother, broke into a smile. 'Aye, Mrs Baird, thank ye.'

Once they were all settled with hot milk and tablet, Helen went on to explain her concerns.

'The worry, Flora, is that the factor, Mr Adam, wants us out of Wee Garclaugh. He's bin on at James for a while that he's not doing enough on the farm. The tenancy runs out next month and we are afraid that with the laird gone, he will put us out. Last time the tenancy came up James managed to persuade the laird to give us a wee bit longer. He only gave us a seven-year lease, rather than the eleven years that we were expecting, and it's about to run oot. Do you ken who the new laird will be?'

'We have only heard rumour, Helen. As far as folk ken it will be the nephew. His name is also James. I suppose that we will hear more after the funeral.'

'And when's that, Flora?'

'We haven't heard. It won't be soon, as they will have to leave time for all his kin in England to come north, and in this weather that could tak some time.'

Flora could see that Helen was still distressed, but there was little that she could offer in the way of comfort, especially as she knew that Helen's husband James had not been farming the place well. John had often complained of the state of the fields and the cattle. As far as John was concerned, the factor had good reason to end their tenancy.

'So if you are put oot, what will ye do?' asked Flora.

'That's why I'm fretting, Flora. The older ones have left and are working away, but we will still have the other six.' Helen was starting to look tearful and Flora could see why she had come to visit. She just needed someone to listen to the worries that had been going round and round in her head. Flora felt quite helpless.

'Do you have any kin who can help oot?' Flora asked.

'Oh, we have plenty of kin, but not many who will be able to help oot. I just hope that James will be able to pick up some work in one of the quarries or one of the mines.'

'Will he really want to go down the mines, Helen?'

'No, like most folk he won't. But he will have a family to feed, so he may not have the choice.'

There was a pause during which neither of the women spoke. Helen's eyes flitted around the kitchen as if she were hoping to spot an answer to her troubles. Eventually Flora stood up to give the hint that she felt that the conversation had reached an end.

'Aye, well, Flora. I'll be keeping ye from yer chores. Thanks for the milk and the tablet for Helen.'

Flora tried to give her some reassurance. 'Nothing has happened yet, Helen. It may be that it will not be as bad as you fear.'

'Aye, ye might be right, Flora. But it widnae stop me fretting.'

Helen and wee Helen wrapped themselves up again and went out into the yard. Flora watched them walk away and gave wee Helen a wave when she turned around. It was about time that tenants were given more security against being turfed out of their farms, she mused.

*

Richard had seen his last patient and was tidying away his notes and instruments when Thomas Cluny walked into his room. Dr Cluny paused for a moment and looked around, as if he were looking for something amiss.

'Can I help you, Thomas?' Richard asked.

'No. No,' Dr Cluny replied absent-mindedly. 'Well, yes, you can. Have you heard that there is another measles outbreak over at Craigbank?'

'Yes, I had heard,' Richard replied, still waiting to find out what his employer wanted.

'The problem is, Richard, that these diseases do not follow social boundaries. Anyone coming into contact with ill workers and their families could become infected. It's the same with the other infections like scarlatina and, of course, cholera. I am wondering if there is anything that we can do to help prevent these outbreaks. It's time that we got to grips with these diseases and found cures.'

'I agree, Thomas, but what are you proposing that we do?' asked Richard, increasingly puzzled. When Richard had been studying medicine at Edinburgh University, one of the finest medical universities in the world, there had been some professors who were working to find cures for these types of diseases. Unfortunately, because these diseases predominantly affected the poor, Richard felt that insufficient research was being done. Even Prince Albert had succumbed to cholera, so it was a misplaced policy.

'I am proposing that we go over the Craigbank and the other miners' rows and see if we can offer some medical help.'

'But they won't be able to afford to pay, Thomas,' Richard responded.

'I'm proposing that we give up an afternoon a week and offer our help for no charge.' He paused to allow Richard to fully absorb the proposal, then continued, 'It would, of course, be entirely your decision. I realise that you now have many patients. In fact, considering that you have barely been here a year, you have done a remarkable job of bringing in new patients.' He chuckled. 'Even if most seem to be young women.'

Richard paused as he considered what he was being asked, then replied, 'I think that it is an excellent proposal. I have travelled past the miners' rows previously and some of the children are in a very poor state. I would be keen to provide what help I can.'

Thomas Cluny let out a sigh that he had clearly been holding in for some time, awaiting Richard's response to his proposal. 'That's grand.' He turned and began to leave. When he was at the door he half-turned back. 'I thought that you would agree. Yer a good man.' He gave Richard a look of pride.

*

That evening Richard was invited to join the Craig family for their evening meal. He had chosen to walk to their home, despite the continuing cold winds blowing along the empty streets. He carried a hand lamp, which cast a warm light onto the pavement. It was the only thing remotely warm.

The door of their house was opened by Elizabeth, Margo's younger sister. 'Hello, Dr Robertson. Do come in out of the cold.'

'Thank you, Elizabeth, and please call me Richard, as I have told you many times before.'

Margo appeared behind Elizabeth. 'Hello, Richard. Bettie, go and help Mither with the supper.'

Elizabeth screwed up her face as if Margo had done something disgusting. 'Don't call me Bettie; you know that I hate it. Call me Lizzie.' She stomped off along the corridor to the kitchen.

Margo took Richard's overcoat and Richard extinguished the oil lamp. They went into the parlour, where Mr Craig was sitting in a chair close to the coal fire.

'Ah, come on in, Richard, and warm yourself by the fire. Let me get you a drink to warm you inside as well.'

'Thank you, Mr Craig.' Margo's father had not yet dropped the formality by allowing Richard to call him Alex. Perhaps he was too familiar with being called Mr Craig at the bank.

'Well, it's quite an affair up at the Mansfield Estate. Margo tells me that she saw you in their carriage the other day. I assume that you had been called over to give medical help.'

'Yes, Mr Craig. Dr Cluny was not around, so they asked me to step in.'

'That's quite an honour, to be asked to see to the laird when you have only been in the toon for a short time.'

'Yes, it is. It is only a shame that there was not a lot that I could do to help him.'

'Well, let's hope all the inheritance business gets sorted out quickly, so that the tenants know where they stand.'

'But surely the tenants all have contracts?' asked Richard, thinking of John and Flora's situation. 'It's not likely that they would have their tenancies ended.'

'Yes, you're right. But, with a new laird, you do not know what might happen. In banking we don't like uncertainties. We like stability,' Mr Craig replied. 'Now, I can see that the women have laid the table, so let's sit up and we will eat.'

Richard enjoyed coming up to the Craig house for meals, which he seemed to be doing increasingly. Not only did he enjoy being close to Margo, but he enjoyed the family atmosphere that he had missed for so many years when he was studying at university.

Mr Craig and Richard continued their talk after supper, until it was time for Richard to return to his lodgings. Margo showed him to the door, which Richard opened against a gust of cold wind. Margo put her hand on top of his hand and looked into his eyes in a gesture of intimacy that stirred Richard's heart.

He walked back towards Castle thinking of Margo. He had realised that their relationship was growing at the Hogmanay dance at the Castle Hotel, when they had shared several dances together. However, it was too public a place for Richard to express to Margo how he felt about her and since that evening he had not been able to speak to Margo on her own. He yearned for the summer days when he hoped to be able to walk up the Afton Glen with her, once again.

*

It was the afternoon that Dr Cluny and Richard had chosen to help up at the miners' rows. They travelled up to Craigbank in Dr Cluny's dog cart. Dr Cluny had arranged to meet up with one of the women who lived at Craigbank, who was an unofficial spokesperson for many of the families. Her name was Cath Campbell.

When they saw Cath she appeared a formidable character. She wore a brown woollen dress that was stretched around her broad body, making her look like a large bag of turnips. But it seemed to be mainly muscle producing the bulges through her dress. She had a shawl around her shoulders and was smoking a clay pipe. There were several other women standing behind her who were nearly all holding babies and with other young children at their skirts. Cath's frown looked a permanent expression.

Dr Cluny began the exchange of greetings. 'Good day, Mrs Campbell. This is Dr Robertson, who has offered his services as well.'

Cath grunted something, which Richard assumed was a greeting, but could quite easily have been an expletive.

'Perhaps we could start by having a tour of the cottages, so that the families can recognise us when we visit again,' Dr Cluny suggested.

Cath turned and marched away towards the first row that faced the Burnfoot Road. There were four rows of houses that were arranged in a sort of square, with their fronts to the outside. At the end of each side of the square was a narrow alley, which allowed access to the ground behind the row of cottages.

Although the walls of the row of cottages were made of brick and the roof was slate, the floor was earth, which the residents had covered with rush carpets. The first cottage was home to a family of about ten people, which seemed to be fairly typical. There were only two rooms, one of which was a living room, the other a bedroom. The bedroom had two double beds, which Richard realised must accommodate the ten occupants.

The rooms smelt of damp and in this cold weather the wood fire seemed to make little difference to the temperature. Despite the menfolk spending twelve hours a day down the coal mines, most could not afford to buy coal. They were allowed to take home some riddled coal, the small pieces of coal that fell through the riddle grids that were used to separate the larger pieces of coal from the coal dust. This riddled coal would not last them a whole week, so it was only used on the coldest days.

Richard stood in the doorway, looking at the miserable conditions that the family had to endure. Many of the children had sores on their faces and frequently coughed.

After they had visited all the homes in the row, Richard and Dr Cluny walked down the alley to the back of the houses. There were a number of earth closets set back about ten yards from the houses. One or two of the closets had no doors, and all had a puddle of water and human waste around their base. To reach the inside of the closet it would be necessary to step through this human waste. It was clear that some efforts had been made to drain the water away, as Richard could see that shallow drainage ditches had been scraped into the ground at the back of some of the closets. There were also piles of ash that was being used to cover the waste down the pit. The smell was unbearable and Richard was forced to take out his handkerchief and hold it to his nose. Cath Campbell snorted in derision at his action.

After their tour Dr Cluny and Richard thanked Cath Campbell and the other women. They made arrangements to see the worst of the ill children in one of the homes in the following week. On their way back to town, they were both silent and reflective. Eventually Dr Cluny spoke.

'I thought I knew what to expect, but it was worse. It is no wonder that there is so much illness with these families living in these conditions. Only half of these children will see their fifth birthday, Richard, and many will not even see their first.'

'It is not the illness that we need to treat but the living conditions. Can we not speak to the laird and try to get the conditions improved?' Richard asked, with some desperation in his voice.

'We can try, Richard. Laird Hyslop is the one who put up these buildings and takes the rent. He should take responsibility, particularly as the workers are the ones who dig out his coal. I'll see if I can get a meeting with his factor.'

'What really concerns me, Thomas, is where these families are getting their water. The well that they are using is only a short distance from these closets. Sewage could easily get through the ground to the wells. They have discovered in London that cholera is spread through drinking water. The same could happen here.'

'Aye, you're right, Richard. Let's hope that we don't get cholera around here, then.'

CHAPTER SEVEN

July 1870

John and Flora were woken not long before dawn with the cries of their son, Thomas, who was now nearly three months old. They had him in a cot in their bedroom, so that Flora could easily pick him up and give him a short feed to settle him. The excitement of having their first child had long since dissipated, along with the full night's sleep that they used to enjoy.

John lay in a sleeping position, trying hopelessly to return to sleep. He could hear the birds starting their chorus, so he knew that a new day was beginning and that there were many jobs to be done around the farm, as well as the milking. The sounds of the house waking up came to him, so he forced himself out of bed. He could see the unusual pink dawn light spreading out over the hills. These strange pink sunsets and sunrises had started in the previous week and were a mystery to even the old folk, who could not remember seeing anything of the like.

He pulled on his clothes and gave his face a wash from the bowl on the dresser table. As he left the bedroom and crept along the corridor, he could hear sounds from the bedroom next door. It would be his sister-in-law, Jane, who had come over to help Flora with the new baby. She had been with them for several weeks and John was looking forward to her going back to Back Rogerton Farm, as she was becoming tiresome. John was grateful for the help that she gave Flora, but he could do without the regular advice on how the house and even the farm could be better managed. He wouldn't mind if Jane actually had some experience of managing a house or a farm, but she was unmarried and would likely remain so unless she curtailed her bossy manner.

John had reached the kitchen when he heard Jane coming down the stairs. He made a quick dash for the back door and headed for the closet at the end of the garden. After using the closet he headed off down to the fields to bring in his cows for milking.

The two maids appeared in the kitchen, having dressed rapidly and rushed down the stairs. They had both received the sharp end of Jane Mitchell's tongue over the past weeks. Jessie had been with the Baird family for a couple of years, but Sarah had been employed just before the baby had arrived and at fourteen was still only a child herself.

Jane Mitchell turned to give them one of her stern looks. 'Come along, Jessie, let's get the range lit and the porridge on for Mrs Baird. Sarah, you will need to go up to the well and bring a couple of buckets of water to wash the nappies.'

When Flora came down with Thomas, the kitchen was all ordered and the porridge was hot and ready in the luggies. A mug of hot whey was on the table.

'Now sit yourself down, Flora, and have yer hot whey. I will take Thomas from ye.' Jane reached forward to take the infant from Flora's arms. Flora had long given up trying to argue with her sister, so she just handed Thomas over, not bothering to point out that he had filled his nappy. Jane started to bounce Thomas on her arm, making the contents leak out onto her dress. Jessie could see what was happening and struggled hard to hold back a laugh.

Flora spoke quietly to her sister, also struggling to keep a smile from her face. 'You might want to get his nappy changed before you start bouncing him. You will want to get yourself changed fairly soon as well.'

Jane held Thomas away from herself and gave a shocked gasp as she saw the state of her dress. Jessie stepped forward to take the leaking infant, who had a big smile as if he too were joining in with the mirth.

Later in the morning, after the milking had been finished, Flora went through to the dairy where Maggie McCillan was hard at work cleaning up and preparing to make some cheeses. She had already added the rennet to a large drum of heated raw milk and was now waiting for the curds to form on the top.

'Good morning, Maggie. That looks like a big batch that you are making,' Flora commented.

'Aye, Mrs Baird. The cheese room is getting empty, so I need to start getting some more chessets filled.'

'Well, the cheese room is getting empty because everyone seems to want to buy your cheeses. John was just saying the other day that he could turn all the milk from the coos into your Dunlop cheese and stop sending the rest up to Glasgae.'

Maggie chuckled. 'Well, he would have to get some more help in here, then.'

'Has Sarah been of any help to you, Maggie?' Flora asked.

'She's willing, but having not grown up on a farm she doesn't even know how to carry a bucket without spilling it and is so nervous around the coos. The coos can sense it and then start playing up.'

'Well, we want you to learn her how to make the cheeses.' Flora turned to leave, then paused and turned back to Maggie with a conspiratorial smile on her face. 'I have heard rumours about you and a young man, Maggie. I hope that it won't mean that you might be leaving us soon.'

'Aye, well, not all rumours are true, Mrs Baird,' Maggie replied in a very non-committal manner, returning her attention to the cheese-making.

'I notice that you haven't really said yes or no. Anyway, I'm not one to spread gossip. It's your own business, but you will tell us if this becomes a serious relationship, won't ye? We would have to make plans for another dairy maid, and how we would replace you I do not know. You have been with us since we first moved into Garclaugh. You are like one of the family, even though you insist on calling me Mrs Baird, rather than Flora.'

Maggie laughed. 'Aye, I'll let you know if any keen man comes calling on me, Mrs Baird.'

*

John was in one of the calf pens inspecting the young bull that had been born back in April, at about the same time as his son. Flora had teased him that he seemed more concerned about the birth of a prize bull calf than that of his own child. John thought proudly about his baby son and how he would teach him about breeding good Ayrshire cows.

It was John's ambition to breed a prize-winning Ayrshire herd, and the bull calf could be the start of this journey. Its dam was a champion Ayrshire cow that he had bought from a farm near Mauchline, whilst its sire was a bull owed by his brother Thomas at South Blairkip. This bull had a good pedigree, having been bred by John's own father. John had been only fifteen when his father had passed on, so he had mainly learned about cows from his brother.

His daydreaming was broken by a man's voice outside the pen.

'Guid morning, Mr Baird. What are we on to today?' It was James McCleon, his ploughman.

'Guid morning, James,' John replied. 'I want you to turn the hay in the bottom meadows. Hopefully this sunshine will continue and we can start to fetch it in this afternoon. I'll send a message across to Andrew Houston and find out if he can spare the men.'

As Helen Houston had feared, the factor at Mansfield House had refused to renew James Houston's lease and the family had had to move out. Lady Jane, who was acting as the new laird in the absence of her late husband's nephew, had proposed that the expelled family move into one of the cottages that had recently been vacated. The new lease for Wee Garclaugh Farm had been given to Andrew Houston, who was James's cousin. Andrew Houston was only a few years younger than John Baird and the two men had quickly formed a good working relationship. They had agreed to share the hiring of two workers at the May Fair for the summer season. Since the farms were next door to each other it was easy for the workers to swap between the two whenever they were required.

'Did you see the sky this morning, Mr Baird?' asked James.

'Aye, it was very strange, wasn't it? I dinnae ken if it means that we will get guid weather or lots of rain.'

John returned to the house to send Jessie off with a note to Wee Garclaugh. As he was about to leave he spotted William Barbour, the post runner, coming down the drive.

'Just hang on here, Jessie. We might save you a run,' John said.

William Barbour was one of two post carriers in New Cumnock, the other being John Gibson. They would walk, or often run, the post for John McCellan, the postmaster, from the post office near the station to all the addresses around the town. They would even run letters to the hill farms up at Cairn and High Polquheys. It was convenient that they were also shoemakers, as their boots would often need repairing.

'Guid marning, Mr Baird,' William Barbour announced in a loud voice, as if John were standing at the other side of the yard. 'I have a telegram for ye that Mr McLellan said was urgent.'

'Thank you, Will. Would ye be going on to Wee Garclaugh?' John asked.

'I wasn't, but I will take a letter over for you if ye wish.'

'No, Will, there's no need to go oot yer way.' John turned to Jessie. 'Off you go, Jessie, see if you can keep up with Will as he walks up the drive. He'll walk as fast as you can run.'

Will set off with Jessie running up behind, giggling at the competition that she had been given. John returned to the house to open the telegram.

He sat at the kitchen table and slit open the telegram with a knife. It was bad news. His mother, Christina Clark, had died at her home in Sanquhar. She was eighty years old and had been poorly for nearly a year, so it was not a big surprise to John.

Flora came into the kitchen from the dairy. She could see from John's face, and the telegram that he held in his hand, that something bad had happened.

'Is it yer mither, John?'

'Aye, she's gone. At least she is not suffering any more.' He paused, staring absent-mindedly in front of him. 'It was guid that we took wee Thomas to see her before she got really bad. I'll contact Hugh and William to find out if they need any help with the arrangements. We could offer to put some of the family up here, if need be.'

'Aye, John. I'll explain to Jane that we will need her room and that she will need to head off back to Back Rogerton. I'll get the girls to clean up the room and their room. They can go sleep in the byre loft whilst the family are here.' Flora left the kitchen to find her sister.

'Poor Chrissie. She spent the last ten years looking after Mither. I wonder what she will do now. At thirty-six she's almost too old to marry,' John murmured to himself. He then registered what Flora had said about her sister leaving and he cheered up greatly.

John had eight siblings, five brothers and three sisters, although his elder brother Gilbert had died in 1842 at only twenty years old. Younger brother William now lived in Sanquhar, as did his twin sister Christina, or Chrissie, and their youngest brother Hugh. Hugh was a teacher, and Christina and their mother had lived with him in the school house.

*

Later that week, after Jane Mitchell had left for the station, the two housemaids Jessie and Sarah were busy cleaning the bedroom in preparation for John's sister Mary and her children, who would be visiting for the funeral. Flora was outside in the kitchen garden seeing what vegetables were ready to be harvested for meals. She had planted a new type of bean, called French beans, which she was keen to pick and eat. She was pleased to see that there were plenty of these pods ready. She added these to the basket of peas that she had already picked.

Although Sarah had collected eggs from the hen house in the morning, Flora had another look and found that two more had been laid. She also checked on the broody hen that was in a separate part of the hen house. She was contentedly sitting on the clutch of twelve eggs that Flora had put under her for hatching into chicks.

As Flora was returning to the house she heard someone calling and turned to see her new neighbour Grace Houston coming around the end of the barn into the kitchen garden, along with her daughter Mary, who was about three years old.

'Hello there, Flora,' Grace called. She looked happy, brushing back her long auburn hair as the slight breeze pushed strands over her face. 'How are ye today?'

'I'm fine, thank you, Grace, and how are you?'

'I'm in guid fettle. In fact, I'm in more than guid fettle; I'm in excellent fettle,' Grace replied.

'Well, that's some confession,' Flora said, laughing. 'What has brought about this excellent condition?'

'The sun is shining and the farm work is going well. I thought that I would walk over with Mary and see how things are going with you. How is wee Thomas?'

'Thomas is fine. He has been having a nap and I'll be waking him soon.' Flora bent down to speak to Mary. 'Would ye like to see the wee bairn, Mary?'

Mary's face broke into a smile and she looked up at her mother for confirmation that this was allowed.

Flora stood up and collected her basket of vegetables and eggs. 'Let's go indoors and we will get ye something to eat and drink. I might have some bannocks in the cupboard.'

The two women and little Mary walked down the path and entered the door to the back place. They went into the kitchen and Flora motioned Grace to sit down. Mary stood next to her mother, playing with the hair that hung down to her shoulders.

'I'll just go to the bedroom and fetch wee Thomas.'

Flora came down holding Thomas, who was looking around him in a bewildered manner, having just woken up.

'Aah. He's a bonnie wee lad, Flora,' Grace remarked.

Flora squatted down so that Mary could see Thomas. 'Ye'll be having a bairn in yer house in the new year, Mary. Do ye want a new brother or a sister?'

'I already have a brother, George. I want a sister next,' Mary replied.

Flora and Grace laughed. 'Well, we will just have to see what God brings us, Mary.'

Flora called for Sarah to come and change Thomas' nappy. Grace and Flora then continued to talk about their children and the farm, whilst Mary tried to amuse Thomas, who gurgled on his back in his basket.

Grace leaned over to get Flora's attention and spoke. 'Andrew was reading the *Advertiser* last evening. He says that there is talk about the price of wheat falling because of all this corn that is coming over from America. If it brings the price of flour and bread down, then there will not be many folks complaining. There will be plenty of the big farms over towards Ayr that will be worried, though; there is a lot of wheat grown over there.'

'Aye, John was saying that there was a lot of talk about it at the last market,' Flora replied. 'As ye say, it should not affect us too much. We don't grow wheat and we use all of our oats for feeding the animals.'

There was a pause whilst they watched Mary trying to get Thomas to grab her fingers.

'I was reading that all these pink skies are caused by fires over in Canada, would ye believe?' Grace asked. 'The smoke from the fires must have drifted right across the ocean. They have had a drought over there and the grass has caught fire.'

'Wheesht!' exclaimed Flora. 'It must have been some big fire to have caused that much smoke. I hope that nobody has been hurt. There have been some folk that John knows who have emigrated out to Canada. The government have been offering a lot of farmland for a very cheap price to encourage farmers to go over there.'

'Fancy uprooting yerself from yer family and going off to live in a country at the other side of the world.' Grace paused thoughtfully. 'But, if ye have lost everything, it must be a temptation. I know that James felt very bad when he lost Wee Garclaugh. He's gone from a farmer to a labourer. But ye need the money to get over to Canada, and I can't see him ever getting that.'

'If a man can go over to Canada and farm his own land, rather than the laird's, it is a big temptation, even if it means leaving yer family behind,' Flora mused.

Their conversation was disturbed by Thomas starting to wail after having his nappy changed. Flora picked him up to soothe him.

'Aye, well, Flora, it's been nice getting oot the hoose for a while. I'll need to get back and get supper sorted for the men. They've been fetching in the hay. The two men that John and Andrew have hired are guid workers. Andrew has been talking about persuading one of them to stay on over the winter, but they want to get work on the tatties.' Grace bent down to take Mary's hand. 'Come on now, Mary, say goodbye to Thomas and thank Mrs Baird for the bannock and the whey.'

With Thomas in her arms, Flora followed Grace and Mary through the door into the yard. She could hear the cows coming in for their milking and the clatter of milk churns as Maggie prepared the dairy. Swallows and house martens were squealing through the air and disappearing into the open shed doors to feed their growing young with the insects that the cows had disturbed walking up from the meadows. Flora hugged Thomas and waved to Mary as their neighbours walked back to their home. She felt happy.

*

The summer continued to bring warm weather that made the grass grow, the crops ripen and the lambs in the hills fatten up. Whilst the farm workers stripped off their clothes to work bare-chested in the fields under the hot sun, the miners toiled underground. They would only see the setting sun as they trudged back to the meagre meals that their wives would have prepared for them. Existing pits were being expanded and new pits were being dug as the demand for coal from the cities grew. New Cumnock found itself expanding as workers from England and Ireland moved into the area to take up the new jobs on offer. Even highlanders driven off their land to make way for sheep had come south to find work.

Dr Cluny's practices in New Cumnock and in Ayr were growing and Richard's list of patients had increased considerably, as had his reputation in town. He was a regular visitor at the Craig household and Alex Craig treated him almost like the son that he had never had. Richard valued his walks with Margo up the Afton valley, as their friendship developed into passion.

One afternoon Richard and Margo were resting in the grass next to the river, whilst Margo's sister Lizzie collected wild flowers to take back to her mother. Richard propped himself up on one elbow and turned to look at Margo. The sun shone through her hair, making it look like golden threads. Margo wiped strands from her face and leaned forward to kiss Richard gently on the lips. Richard desperately wanted to devour her whole being, but he restrained himself and pulled back from her. Margo looked at him, puzzled.

'What is it, Richard?' she asked, with worry and confusion in her tone.

'You need to know more about my background, Margo, before our relationship goes any further.'

So Richard began to explain his upbringing and the good fortune that had brought him out of poverty to the position he now held as a young town doctor in a well-respected practice. When he had finished Margo was sitting up, looking into his eyes.

'That's quite a story, Richard, but you tell it as if it is something of which you should be ashamed. Just because your faither was a labourer and a drunkard does not make you less of a man. You have suffered a tragic childhood, not least having to watch your mither being beaten by your faither. No wain should have to suffer in that way.' She paused and looked down at the ground. Her sister came dancing across the grass holding a bunch of flowers.

'Just look at all these bonnie flowers, Richard. Mither is going to love them,' Lizzie exclaimed. Her arrival broke Margo's reflection on Richard's story. She looked up at her sister, shading her eyes against the sun that was shining on her face.

'Aye, they're bonnie, Lizzie. Let's get them wrapped up so that they still look as bonnie when we get them hame.' Margo pushed herself up and took a moment to lay her hand on Richard's arm, giving him a loving smile and a look of reassurance.

CHAPTER EIGHT
February 1871

Listening, the doors and windows rattle.
I thought me on the shivering cattle.

'A Winter Night', Robert Burns

It had been a long, cold winter. Snow had covered the hills since mid-November and a cold north wind had blown down the Nith valley, freezing everything in its path. The only people who were glad of the cold were the champion curling team who spent many hours on the ice at Lochside, ready to defend the Eglington Jug that they had won the previous year. John had gone along for a few games, but he was not as skilful as some and lacked the enthusiasm to practise often.

The cold brought problems in the dairy, freezing the milk left in the churns. Maggie and Flora had worked hard to turn as much of the milk into cheese as possible, as the town dairies would not buy milk that had been frozen.

The cows themselves were kept in the byre over the winter. They were fed with the hay that had been collected during the previous summer, supplemented with milled oats and chopped turnips. John had also bought in some molasses to give the cows some extra food. The cows loved the sweet molasses and pushed each other to get to the black treacle-like substance that was poured out into their feed troughs. Molasses are a waste product from the sugar industry and contain many vitamins that are good for the cattle. Unlike the sweet-tasting molasses that are a by-product of making sugar from cane, the molasses that farmers use for cattle feed comes from the sugar beet industry and is unpalatable to humans.

John kept a close eye on the amount of hay and other foods that he had available for the cows. If the winter lasted too long then they would not want to run out of fodder for the cattle.

Richard Robertson came to visit John and Flora on his newly acquired horse. Having struggled to get around to his patients using Dr Cluny's trap, he had decided that the easiest form of transport would be a horse. He had been persuaded to buy one from a horse breeder in Old Cumnock, not far to the north.

John was busy taking hay to the calf pens when Richard rode into the yard. John finished putting hay into the ricks in the pens and walked across to join Richard, who had dismounted using the stone blocks set into the side of the south barn.

'Bye, that's a guid horse you've got yerself there, Richard,' John said admiringly. He patted its rump and ran his hand down its legs. The horse shivered and chewed at the bit in its mouth.

The more that John examined the horse, the more impressed he was. 'You must have paid a lot of money for this one, Richard,' he said, whilst examining the horse's teeth.

'I didn't think that I had paid a large sum. A number of folk have made the same comment. I just wanted a reliable horse that would get me safely around the countryside,' Richard defended himself.

'This is a race horse, not a doctor's horse, Richard. You will need to enter it in the Castle Races.' John chuckled and put his hand on Richard's shoulder. The two men had formed a good friendship since they had first met two years previously. 'Now come inside and we will get you some hot milk.' He took Richard towards the back door that led into the warmth of the kitchen.

Flora had seen Richard arrive and had already got Sarah to put a pan of whey on the range.

'Come on in, Richard, and warm yerself,' Flora greeted Richard as he walked into the kitchen. 'I'll leave you with Flora just a while, as I have to finish feeding the cattle,' John explained as he disappeared from the doorway.

Richard took off his overcoat and settled on a chair in front of the range that was stacked with coal and radiated heat like a furnace. Flora finished feeding Thomas, who was on her lap and staring at Richard with his big blue eyes. She wiped his face and carefully lifted him down so that he stood on his wobbly legs, clinging on to her skirt. He was still staring suspiciously at Richard.

'He's doing well, Flora. It won't be long before he is walking on his own.'

'No, you're right. John and I keep encouraging him to take a step, but he's just ten months, so there is no rush. Anyway, I keep being told by other mothers that it is much easier when they stay where you leave them.' Flora laughed.

Thomas eventually plopped down onto his bottom and crawled away under the table, where he had spotted some dropped bread.

'So, to what do we owe this call, Richard?' Flora enquired. 'Were you up this way anyway?'

'I've just been calling on Grace Houston to check on the bairn.'

'Aye, she's a bonnie wee lassie. How's she getting on?'

'Wee Jane is fine, but Grace is not well and has a fever. John is quite worried, which is why they sent me a message. Grace didn't have an easy birth, so we have to see how the fever progresses.'

'Her sister was staying a while after the bairn was born. Is her sister still there?' Flora asked, clearly concerned.

'Aye. Her sister is still there and is a great help to Grace and John,' Richard replied.

At this point the back door opened and a draught of cold air blew through to the kitchen. John's voice came through to Flora and Richard. 'Bye, I'm sure that wind has picked up this morning. It's enough to freeze yer lips together.'

John removed his overcoat and came through to stand with his back close to the range. 'You should see the horse that Richard's got tied up outside, Flora. It's a braw horse.'

Flora looked out of the window into the yard, trying to spot it. She then turned to Richard. 'Is it yours, Richard?'

'Aye, but I am beginning to regret buying it as everyone seems to think that I should turn it into a race horse,' he replied. 'I bought it as a pack horse to get me and my bag around the hills.'

'Well, it could do both, Richard. I was telling him, Flora, that he will have to ride it in the Castle Races.' John chuckled at his own remark.

Richard laughed. 'You must remember that I watched the Castle Race last year. That wasn't a horse race; it was a circus. I don't want to end up in Dr Cluny's surgery like some did afterwards.'

'Well, perhaps you could get someone else to ride it for you,' suggested John.

'Och, John, just let him be,' Flora interrupted. 'Now how's Margo?'

'Margo is fine and sends her regards.'

'I saw her a couple of weeks ago when I was up at the shops at Castle,' Flora said. 'She was telling me that you are helping up at the miners' rows. Who's paying you to do the work there?'

'Dr Cluny and I are giving medical help where it is needed. The miners have given us some payment and we have even been given some bags of coal that they have collected from the waste tips. Even though they are poor, they don't want to be seen as receivers of charity. They are a proud bunch. But it is very distressing seeing the illnesses and the injuries, even in the children. Did you know that despite the Mines Act of 1842 there are still children as young as eleven working down the mines as trappers? They sit at the doors or traps on the tram tracks and when they hear a tram coming they open the door, and when it has passed they close it. They sit there in the damp and the pitch dark, with rats running about and water dripping on their heads. It's appalling. When I have spoken to the mothers they say that the money these children bring in can be the difference between the family going hungry or not.'

'Aye, well, until they brought in the Colliery Act they used to have children under ten working down mines. Have you tried speaking to Mr Hyslop, the mine owner at Bank?' John asked.

'Dr Cluny and I have both tried to get a meeting, but as soon as we say that it is about the conditions of the miners' cottages, we are told it is not possible to speak to the laird. We got to speak to the manager, who listened to the points that we raised, then said that he would pass on our comments to the laird. We both came out of the meeting thinking that that would be the last we would hear about it. Sure enough, neither of us has received any reply from the manager or the laird.'

Richard paused, and John and Flora looked at each other. It was clear that Richard was getting quite upset just talking about it. Flora spoke first.

'I am sorry that I mentioned the mines, Richard. I dinnae want to upset ye.'

'No, it's fine, Flora,' Richard replied, but it was clear that there was plenty more that he wanted to get off his chest. 'You can imagine what those cottages are like in this weather. The floors are just packed earth, so the damp just comes up into where the children are sleeping and living. As I walk along the rows you can hear the coughing of these children. They are doing very well if they reach five years of age without a serious illness, and where they live so close together diseases just spread through families. I have tried to get them to boil water for drinking, but some families barely have enough wood to heat their food.' He paused again; he could see that John and Flora were shocked. 'I'm sorry. I didn't come over here to give you a lecture on the living conditions of the miners and their families.'

'No, that's fine, Richard,' John responded. 'It's interesting what you say about the water. I am worried about my coos all cramped together in the byre over the winter. That's when cattle diseases start up and can spread. We are lucky that we have a good well here on the farm. The water is always clear with no taste. We have also got the Blubber Well spring over in the next field, which gives clean water throughout the year, even when there is a drought. With the river being so polluted with sewage, I am minded to fence off the river and make sure that the coos only drink the water from Blubber Well. What do you think, Richard?'

'I think you would be wise to do that. I have wondered myself if any diseases get from the river into the milk that way. What we really need to do is clean up the river so that everyone in the town can get clean water for drinking and washing.'

'Well, that will take a lot of time and money, Richard,' John said. 'Why don't you start a campaign in the town?'

'I might just do that,' Richard said with a chuckle, his anger now much reduced.

The three friends continued to talk easily of their plans and the news of the world that had reached them through the *Ayr Advertiser*. Richard was an avid reader and would often tell John and Flora of snippets of news that he had read. John was more interested in the price that milk and meat fetched in the cities and the effects of the grain trade from Canada and America, whilst Richard followed the politics of the times and the campaigns to improve the living conditions of workers around

Great Britain. But, as always, it was the home issues that occupied the time and interest of them all: Flora helping her young son take his first steps, John tending to his much-loved cows and his prize bull calf, and Richard deciding when to ask Margo to be his wife.

CHAPTER NINE

April 1871

The cold winter eventually receded and warmth returned to the Nith valley. The cows had, at last, been allowed out onto the pastures, after four months confined in the byre. They ran across the grass and pranced with delight, like prisoners released from captivity, their udders swinging from side to side in a most ungainly manner. John watched with pleasure, looking forward to another year when he could grow his herd of Ayrshire cows and show his family that he could continue the fine reputation of the Bairds as dairy farmers.

Richard had at last plucked up courage to ask Margo for her hand in marriage and then taken the nervous steps to the door of the Craig family home to seek permission from her father. Margo had persuaded Richard to spare no details of his past when talking to her father, and her faith in her father was rewarded when he stepped forward to shake Richard by the hand and call him 'son'. Richard was flushed with various emotions, as he felt as if he had found a proper father, as well as a wife.

The marriage was fixed for late April. Dr Cluny had arranged for Richard to move into the upper rooms in the practice house, now that his own son had moved out to live in Ayr.

At the neighbouring farm of Mansfield Mains, Jack Picken had also let his cows out onto the grass fields and was walking amongst them as they grazed. He had noticed that a couple of the cows had seemed quite listless that morning and were walking as if their feet were sore. He wondered if the long winter had caused some hoof rot.

One of the two cows that were causing him concern was standing quietly trying to chew some grass. Jack noticed that it was drooling foam from its mouth. He felt a shiver go up his back. This did not look like just bad feet. He walked back to the steading thoughtfully and called to his worker Peter.

'Peter, give me a hand to bring a couple of coos into the yard,' he instructed.

Jack and Peter returned to the field of grazing cows and herded the two cows back to the farm yard. They took one of the cows into a small pen and pushed it against the wall, so that Jack could inspect the cow's mouth. There was no doubt. The cow's gums had painful blisters, and as Jack ran his hand down the front leg to its hoof the cow winced and lifted its foot. Jack did not need a veterinarian to tell him that it was foot and mouth disease. He released the cow and stood back looking at it, as he absorbed the consequences of what he had just discovered. He would have to inform the local vet and the authorities. The Contagious Diseases (Animals) Act brought out in the previous year had made this a requirement. But first Jack went into his house to pour himself a whisky.

*

News of the foot and mouth disease at Mansfield Mains spread quickly. The local vet had confirmed the diagnosis and plans were now being made to slaughter all of Jack Picken's herd. The disease was highly infectious and there was no cure. Any animals that recovered were severely disabled and useless as milk cows. The farmers in the area called it *murrain*: death.

The farm was isolated, as were all the surrounding farms. This, of course, included Garclaugh. This would mean that they would not be able to move cows out of the farm and would also mean that visitors to Garclaugh would have to be restricted.

John and Flora sat in their kitchen, stunned by the news.

'What are you going to do, John? How can we keep the coos safe from the murrain?'

'I'll graze the herd in the fields furthest from the boundary with Mains. There should be enough grazing in the river meadows. I'll put a gate at the top of the track and make sure that no visitors come to us through Mansfield. Perhaps I should put a bucket of carbolic for folk to wash their hands and feet.'

'But what aboot getting the milk churns to the station and the children going to school?' Flora asked.

'We'll use the track doon past Merkland. It's a longer journey, but it will take us well away from the Mains. Or perhaps we should keep oor coos indoors and wait for their cattle to be killed and burned?'

Flora watched her husband's face as he struggled through all these thoughts, there being little comfort that she could offer. John had spent the past four years building up his herd and now all his hard work could disappear.

The next day John and Flora could hear the animals in the Mains being shot. A wagon had brought stacks of wood to build a pyre for the dead animals. Jack Picken's sheep were left on the hillside, but he was told that he must not cross the road to visit them. His neighbours, who also had sheep on the slopes, would watch out for any sign of the disease.

After the initial shock of the outbreak, questions started to be asked as to how the infection had reached New Cumnock. There had been various outbreaks in England recently, but there had not been an outbreak in Scotland for some years. At the end of long winters, farmers often bought in extra fodder to supplement their diminishing supplies. This was believed to be the most likely way that the infection had arrived at Mansfield Mains. Not that this was of any comfort to the Picken family, who watched their livelihood going up into the sky as the pyres were lit and the diseased carcasses were cremated.

The smell of the pyres hung around in the valley for many days. There was a sombre atmosphere around Garclaugh. Even the birds seemingly stopped their songs and moved away to hunt elsewhere for the insects to feed their young. All the neighbouring farmers were waiting anxiously for any sign of the dreaded murrain in their livestock. No animals were allowed to leave the farms and John was relieved that most of his milk was being used to make cheese, which meant that he did not have to travel to town each day to put churns onto the train. Maggie had decided to move into the farmhouse for a while, so that she did not have to walk from Pathhead each morning, passing the Mains. She shared a room with Jessie and Sarah.

One morning Flora went into the dairy to help Maggie and found her leaning over a bucket, retching.

'Dear me, Maggie, what's up?' Flora rested her hand on Maggie's shoulder as she continued to retch.

Eventually Maggie straightened up. 'I dinnae ken, Flora. I have felt queasy for the last couple of mornings.'

Flora took her hand off Maggie's shoulder.

'Maggie,' she said quietly, 'are your courses late?'

Maggie turned to Flora. Flora could tell the answer to her question from the look on Maggie's face.

'Oh, Maggie, Maggie. Who's got you in this condition? Is it this man that you have been seeing?'

Maggie buried her face in her hands and sobbed. She tried to wipe her face with her cloth, but still the tears flowed.

Flora rested her hand on her shoulders. 'Do you want to come inside and sit doon?'

'No, no. I dinnae want Jessie and Sarah seeing me like this. There's enough gossip going around anyway,' Maggie choked out between sobs.

After a while Maggie's sobs subsided and she wiped her face and tidied away the bucket that she had been using. Flora stood watching, at a loss for what to say to her.

Eventually, Flora spoke. 'You'll need to tell this young man, Maggie. You will need to arrange a marriage.'

'Well, that's not going to be easy, Flora, because he has gone to work down in England. This is the result of oor last night together before he left,' Maggie explained. 'He promised to come back and visit later in the year. He said that he would write to me with his new address once he has found lodgings.'

'Well then, Maggie, I'm sure that that will be soon and you will be able to tell him your news.'

'Aye, it's possible. But how long can I keep my condition quiet?' Maggie asked herself, as much as asking Flora.

'Well, we will just have to manage as best we can, Maggie. You'll have my help.'

'Thank you, Flora,' Maggie replied softly, struggling to hold her emotions in check.

Maggie turned and returned to her work in the dairy, and Flora left to ponder what would happen. Maggie would have to leave at some stage as her pregnancy became more obvious. Flora knew that the kirk folk would judge Maggie badly. Maggie was with the Free Church and, although they no longer made fallen women sit on a stool in the kirk to be humiliated, there would be universal disapproval. What would become of their cheeses? Maggie was one of the best makers of Dunlop cheeses in the valley, if not *the* best. Maggie had been teaching Sarah how to make cheeses, but Sarah was still a long way from becoming proficient.

John was not impressed when Flora told him about Maggie's condition.

'What? How could she be such a tawpie? This man will not come back,' exclaimed John.

'Well, it's happened and we just have to deal with it.'

'I've a mind to send her on her way today,' John said.

'You'll do nae such thing, John Baird. Where's your Christianity?'

'She's the one who should be thinking about God's laws. She'll be labelled a fornicator down at the Free Kirk.'

'Aye, which is even more reason that we should give her some support. It's not as if she has much support at her home. Her faither will probably put her oot the hoose,' Flora said.

'Of all the times for this to happen,' John muttered. 'What with the murrain to worry us, and now we will lose our dairy maid. How is Sarah getting on larnin' in the dairy?'

'Slowly, John, slowly. Perhaps if she worked in there all the time with Maggie, then she would get on larnin' faster.'

'Aye. Well, let's just get on and do that. Will you miss her around the hoose?' John asked.

'No. Now that Thomas is easier to manage, Jessie and I can get on with the jobs without Sarah.'

'Aye. Well, let's just get on with it. There's no point in fretting,' John said, as he stood to get his coat and return to the many tasks around the farm. Flora went to seek out Sarah and tell her to spend more time in the dairy learning to be a dairy maid. Life on the farm would carry on, despite the farming and personal dramas.

CHAPTER TEN

June 1873

By Mauchline Race or Mauchline Fair,
I should be proud to meet you there.

'Epistle to J Lapraik', Robert Burns

After two wet summers, the farmers around New Cumnock were hoping that it would not be a third poor harvest. However, this hot summer had followed on from a warm spring and all seemed to look promising for a good year on the farms. The worries about the foot and mouth outbreak seemed a long time in the past. The infection had not spread beyond Mansfield Mains and the area was declared all clear by the end of that November. John Baird's dairy herd had continued to grow and he was now producing some excellent Ayrshire heifers and bull calves that were fetching good prices at the markets.

Cheese making had returned, through the work of a now proficient Sarah Campbell, to the level it had reached when Maggie McCillan was working for the family. Maggie's young man had indeed returned from England and taken her to be his wife. Flora had received letters from Maggie describing their lovely daughter, who was now running around their cottage in Wales. Maggie's husband worked as a manager in one of the Welsh coal mines, having learned his skills in the pits of Ayrshire. Flora wondered if Maggie would be teaching the local Welsh dairy maids how to make Dunlop cheese.

Richard and Margo were now settled into their new home above the surgery and Margo had given birth to a healthy girl, Jane, who was now just over a year old. Flora had also given birth to a daughter, called Mary. She was named after Flora's mother, which was the tradition in Scotland, the first son being named after the father's father and the first daughter after the mother's mother.

Dr Cluny's practice was progressing well now that Richard was well established and had gained a formidable reputation around the town. The story of his childhood years was now known to his friends, and many others knew that he had come from humble stock. His lack of a suitable family and useful connections may have been a problem in England, but in Scotland people were more likely to be judged by their actions and their character than their breeding. He was fortunate that his intelligence had been spotted early by a teacher who had given him extra lessons. Later, that same teacher had brought Richard to the attention of a wealthy, but childless, Dumfries resident who informally adopted Richard and paid for his university training. But his hard childhood in a poor household with an abusive father had given Richard a burning desire to improve the circumstances of ordinary working families. Families like those at Craigbank and the other growing miners' village at Connel Park were now well used to his visits and treated him with great respect.

Dr Cluny and Richard had not made much progress in improving the conditions in the miners' villages, but there were small victories. Richard had managed to get improved toilets built at Craigbank, but he still had a lot of concerns about the water supply and the dreadful state of the rivers. So when the local council were required, by the new water board, to establish a sub-committee to consider how to provide clean water to the residents of New Cumnock, Dr Robertson's name was one of the first that was written on the list of possible members.

Richard eagerly accepted the offer to join the group and help turn his plans into reality. Some thought that the idea of bringing water to New Cumnock was a waste of time, when there were already two rivers. However, the council brought in a water engineer from Edinburgh and an investigation was started to find suitable sources of clean water that could be piped into the town. Richard was enthusiastic and excited. Unfortunately, his optimism was to wane as the meetings and investigations were to drag on for three years without a single pipe being laid.

*

One afternoon Dr Cluny called Richard into his room for a meeting. Richard was not particularly surprised, as they often met to discuss medical cases or the work that they were doing at the miners' rows. But he did find himself very surprised when he was offered a partnership in Dr Cluny's practice.

Dr Cluny paused and waited for a response from Richard.

'Well, that is a surprising and interesting offer,' Richard managed to say, after a long, thoughtful pause.

'I was hoping for a little more enthusiasm, Richard.'

'I'm sorry, Thomas. There is a lot going through my mind. In particular I am wondering how much you will require to join the practice and what your son in Ayr will have to say about me joining as a partner.'

'You are quite right, Richard, these are important questions. Firstly, my son has a successful practice in Ayr and has made it very clear to me that he is not interested in this practice. If anything were to happen to me, he tells me that he would sell it. Secondly, I am aware that you have not got access to the capital needed to buy into the practice immediately, but I am happy for you to pay in instalments over a number of years. Perhaps your father-in-law might help you get a loan from the Glasgow Bank?' Thomas Cluny paused and watched Richard consider these options. 'You take some time, Richard, and think on it.'

'I will, Thomas, and I am very grateful for this opportunity you have offered.' Richard stood up and shook Thomas' hand.

Later that evening Richard told Margo of the offer that he had been presented with. It would mean that he would be able to help develop the practice and have a stable future in the town. They decided to approach Margo's father in order to find out if they could get a loan. This was soon done. Alex Craig was delighted to help arrange the loan, and soon Richard was able to become a full partner in the practice. Richard and Margo stood admiring the new brass plate that had appeared by the front door of the practice house, announcing Richard's elevated status.

New Cumnock was also growing in status as more money flowed into the town. The coal mines had expanded and this had brought work for blacksmiths, farriers, carters, bakers and many other trades that had opened new businesses in town. A new clock had been installed in the church tower, whose faces could be seen from four directions. Even the curling team had added to the reputation of New Cumnock by winning the Eglington Jug three years in a row.

Ready to deliver churns of milk to the station.
Courtesy of Terry Harrison

New train tracks were being laid to the various pitheads in order to take the wagons of coal to their destinations around Scotland and beyond. Many went to the ports on the west coast of Ayrshire, such as Troon. The farms around the town expanded to satisfy the demand for dairy produce in Glasgow and a special train ran every morning with churns of fresh milk, and boxes of cheese and butter. It was always a race for the dairy farmers to get the steel churns to the station before the train left. John Baird had done this transporting countless times and had watched the train rattle off northwards to its next stop at Old Cumnock, where more produce would be loaded by porters. It was certainly easier for John to sell his milk to the big dairies than to try to sell it directly to local customers, as some of the other smaller dairy farmers were doing.

*

It was a Wednesday in early June and John, Flora, Thomas and wee Mary were at the station waiting for the train to take them to Cumnock for the Summer Fair. John's uncle William had recently died, so John had decided to combine a trip to Cumnock with a visit to his family at Sorn. John was keen to see what Ayrshire cattle would be on sale, whilst Flora was looking forward to meeting some of her family who were also planning to visit the fair.

The family found a compartment and settled down, with Thomas excitedly climbing on the seats to look out of the window and being chastised by his father for doing so. They would usually take the horse and the dog cart, but John had decided to give his son this special treat. The railway carriages jolted as the train moved off, causing Flora to grab Thomas before he ended up in a heap on the floor.

Now safely on John's lap, Thomas was mesmerised as the buildings appeared to slide past the carriage windows, the clouds of evaporating steam from the engine adding to the mystery. The train gradually increased in speed as it moved onto an embankment, from where they could see the pitheads of the mines in the distance and black smoke belching from the chimney of the smithy on the edge of town. The train was soon passing the glimmering Lochside Loch and then Creoch Loch, thought to be the remnants of a much larger loch that had covered much of the valley floor to the north of the town.

It was only a short journey to Cumnock, and Thomas was disappointed as the train slowed to a stop and the family climbed out of their compartment at the station. Flora's brother James Mitchell was there to meet them, and soon the family were on their way to the market site, where the fair was well underway.

Flora took Thomas and Mary and went off to meet with her mother and her sister Jane, whilst John joined James to meet up with Flora's father Andrew. John found Andrew Mitchell by the pens of Ayrshire cows that were waiting for the sale. Various farmers were examining the cows closely, some having climbed into the pens to open the cows' mouths and examine their teeth. A cow with bad or worn teeth would be unable to eat the grass required to make it a good milker, so a set of good teeth was a vital requirement.

The Ayrshire breed had been developed over a hundred years through crossbreeding with cattle brought over from Holland. The breed was adapted to the harsher conditions in Ayrshire hills and could produce rich milk, even though their pastures were sometimes rough and lacking in nutrition. Prices for good Ayrshire cattle were going up, as more were being taken across to America and even as far as Australia and New Zealand. It was an enterprising time for dairy farmers like the Baird family, who were producing good cows for milking and whose bulls were being sought out for breeding.

It was not long before John was in the midst of a collection of local dairy farmers, including some of his cousins from around Blairkip, passing judgement on the cattle and catching up with family news. These markets provided an important social network to arrange farming business, meet other cattle breeders and do deals.

Flora had found herself in amongst a collection of farmers' wives and family members. She proudly showed off little Mary and struggled to hold on to Thomas as he squirmed under the unwanted attention of his grandmother and aunt. He wanted to be with his father and uncle with the cows.

Eventually Flora, her family and a handful of others left the large group, in order to visit the various stalls that had been set up around the fair. All manner of household goods were on display, including new household devices that had been shipped up from England. There were also a variety of locally made items. One stall sold wooden snuff boxes, for which Cumnock and the nearby town of Mauchline were famous. Another, which caught Flora's attention, was selling straw hats and bonnets. Flora decided that a new hat for herself and a bonnet for Mary would be ideal for the journey up to Blairkip in the hot sun. At least that was how she would justify her purchase to John, who never liked to see money spent.

Thomas was soon tugging at his mother's hand as he spotted some fairground rides. There was a merry-go-round driven by a steam engine, a set of swinging boats and a tall helter-skelter. The bright colours and moving rides were such an attraction for the three-year-old, who could not understand why his mother was pulling him away. He howled with anger and tried to roll onto the grass.

'Now, what's up with you, wee laddie?' a voice asked, and large hands picked him up into the air, stopping his sobs immediately. A surprised Thomas turned to see that his uncle William Mitchell had swept him off the grass. He squealed with delight.

'William!' Flora exclaimed. 'How nice to see you. I didn't know that you would be here as well.' She gave her brother a big hug.

'I managed to persuade the factor that a day at the Cumnock Fair would give me lots of new ideas to take back to Dumfries House.' William worked on the farm of the big estate near Ochiltree, which was owned by the Marquess of Bute. 'The Marquess is keen to set up a model farm for his tenants to learn new agricultural methods, and I have been given the honour of establishing it,' he announced proudly, with a low bow. Some of the unmarried ladies in the group giggled with delight as William was still a bachelor and would be considered a prize catch, particularly with his handsome looks.

'So with your new important position I expect that you will be seeking to settle and find a wife?' William's mother enquired, being very aware of the attention that he was receiving from passing women.

'All in good time, Mither, all in good time. Now let's see which of these wonderful machines is going to entertain my favourite nephew,' he said as he carried wee Thomas towards the fairground rides.

'William always brings a whirl of excitement with him, Mither. I miss him,' Flora mused as she watched him climb onto a wooden horse on the merry-go-round with his arms wrapped around a grinning Thomas.

*

The morning passed by quickly until it was soon gone noon. Flora eventually found John next to the judging ring where the Ayrshire cattle had finished being paraded. Flora had known that John would be in the vicinity, seeing how the cows were being rated for the show awards. He was talking with other dairy farmers about the competition and inevitably there was disagreement between them about which cow was judged the best. The judge had given first prize to a cow from a herd near Kilmarnock, but John and some of the other farmers felt the cow did not have all the features of a good Ayrshire.

'What we need is someone to decide what makes a good Ayrshire cow, otherwise each judge will be using his own ideas, rather than something that has been agreed,' said one farmer.

'My faither still calls them Cunningham cattle and I know of another farmer who calls them Dunlops,' another farmer declared. 'They can't even decide what to call the breed.'

Flora gently touched John's arm. 'John, we will need to make a move if we are to get over to Blairkip for supper time.'

John took his watch from his waistcoat pocket and studied the hour. 'Aye, you're right.' He turned to his fellow dairy farmers. 'Well, gentlemen, I'm going to have to leave you, but we do need to get something sorted about recognising the Ayrshire breed properly.'

John and Flora and the bairns bade their farewells to the Mitchell family members and made their way back to the station to catch a train to Mauchline, where John's brother Tom would meet them with a horse and carriage. Tom was the eldest brother in the family and had inherited the tenancy to the family farm of South Blairkip when their father had died in 1846. When his brother had taken over the tenancy, John had been only fifteen, but it had been clear to him at the time that he would have to find his own farm. Not only had he succeeded, but John felt that he had a better farm at Meikle Garclaugh than South Blairkip.

*

Mauchline station was busy with passengers and with goods trains. As they left the train John could see the bales of cotton being loaded onto wagons for transportation to the cotton mills in Catrine. There seemed to be dozens of wagons and many workers engaged in the task. After greeting his brother in the station yard he mentioned the large number of wagons that were being loaded.

'Well, since the end of the civil war in America the cotton trade has increased and the mills are in full production. In fact they are bringing in workers from Ireland because they are so short of labour to work in the mills,' explained Tom. 'It's been quite a struggle this year to get the summer workers hired. They all seem to want long-term work in the mills, not short-term work on farms.'

'Why would someone choose to work in those factories all day, when they could be out in the sunshine and the fresh air?' asked Flora.

'Aye, well, if it keeps the Irish employed, it will be better than them begging around the farms,' Tom responded, with a touch of annoyance in his voice that suggested he had encountered local beggars and was not at all sympathetic to them. Flora and John looked at each other knowingly, but chose not to take the discussion any further. They both knew that Tom was a man of strong views who did not show much tolerance of anyone who he considered work-shy.

They all climbed into the carriage and set off along the road from Mauchline to Sorn. The road followed a ridge above Catrine, but they could not see the town as it was in the valley to the south. However, they could see the smoke from the various chimneys drifting upwards into the windless sky and then being dragged sideways by an unseen breeze across the upper layers, like paint streaks on a canvas. Evidence of the busy activity in the mills and factories.

The road took them past Sorn Castle, the estate home of Tom's laird, Mr Graham Somervell. John knew that they had a very successful dairy business based there and he strained, unsuccessfully, to see if he could see the steam tractor that he had heard they used to transport wagons of milk churns to the railway station. They then turned north up the Galston road, which would lead to South Blairkip. The road was well made and was bordered by a strip of trees that had been planted alongside most of its eastern length. The sun was still in the sky despite the late hour and the swallows were squealing around catching insects. Cows were grazing busily in the field by the track that led to the farmhouse, the milking having been finished.

The track ended in a yard surrounded on three sides by the steading of single-storey buildings, the byres and the dairy. The farmhouse was attached to and was alongside the back of the steading, with a garden area to its front. Like Meikle Garclaugh it had two storeys with gabled windows, partly in the wall and partly in the roof.

As the carriage passed the farmhouse a stream of children came running out of the front door, jumping and waving at the visitors, followed by Elizabeth, Tom's wife. The children ran into the yard to meet their visitors and there were hugs and greetings all round. The older girls were keen to see baby Mary, whilst the boys tried to entice Thomas away to play. Surrounded by so many unfamiliar children, Thomas clung tightly to his mother's dress and hid his face in its folds.

The two families sat down around a large dining table, some sitting on a sibling's lap, to enjoy the meal that Elizabeth and the older children had helped to prepare. Tempted by the delicious food, Thomas soon overcame his shyness and was laughing along with his cousins, and after the meal he joined in games outside in the evening sunshine. It was a happy scene.

Later that evening Flora joined John in the garden, where he was looking over the burn that flowed in a small valley behind the house.

The setting sun was casting its golden light across the field that sloped upwards away from the steading. Flora ran her arm through John's and hugged him closer. John turned to her and smiled.

'All the children in bed now?' he asked.

'Aye, but how Elizabeth manages with seven children I will never know. Thank goodness Helen is such a help. She seems older than her twelve years. She was so helpful with wee Tom, getting him sorted whilst I was feeding Mary.'

John hugged his wife and stared out again across the fields through which he had walked around earlier, examining the grazing dairy herd with his brother Tom and discussing the merits of the various cows.

'I was just thinking how the Bairds have changed this land in the time that my uncle William has lived. I can remember my faither and him digging all those drainage sheughs until his back was bent and then spreading lime with his bare hands until they were raw and his eyes were burning red. All for sweeter grass for the cows and better crops for feeding his family. It was not surprising that my faither only lived until he was fifty.' John paused and then, with a hint of bitterness in his voice, 'Now another farmer is benefiting from the sweat that he put into that farm, up there on the Campbell land.' John pointed up to the top of the hill where the Coplar farm was situated, close to the Auchmannoch estate house of Robert Campbell, and where John had been born and grew up learning to be a farmer.

'So what age were you when your faither took on South Blairkip, John?' Flora asked.

'I was about twelve. We were only in here a few years before faither passed on. He had so many plans for the farm, especially as the change in the tenancy laws made it easier to stay in a place. In the old times they could have put us all out when faither passed on. Despite all the difficulties his faith was so strong and to him every challenge was God's way of testing that faith. He never let us forget that we were Bairds and we should always make sure that we uphold the good Baird name.'

Tom appeared from the house and shouted across to them. 'Will you come on in for a dram, John, before the sun sets?'

John and Flora went in to join Tom and his wife Elizabeth in the parlour of the South Blairkip farmhouse, where John and his brother talked of breeding cows and Elizabeth and Flora talked of raising children. After such a busy day it was not long before John and Flora made their way upstairs and quietly climbed into bed, trying not to wake the children who were sleeping on hay mattresses on the floor.

*

At breakfast the next morning Elizabeth and her maid were rushing around to get everyone fed. Tom had already risen early to start the milking of the cows and John had gone out to help him. Helen, Elizabeth's eldest daughter, was helping with the little children and was also trying to separate the two three-year-olds, Thomas and his cousin John, who had struck up a rivalry in which each wanted what the other had. Flora and Elizabeth were glad once the older children had gone off to the school and just the younger children were left, giving them time to talk about the new law that would make schooling compulsory for all children at five years old.

'So, Flora,' Elizabeth said, 'have the schools in New Cumnock sorted out how they are going to reorganise to meet the new law?'

'Aye, well, there is going to be a new public school down in toon,' Flora explained. 'They are putting up a new building on land opposite the Old Mill that the Marquess of Bute has donated. This will be the school that wee Tom will attend. So we are hoping that the new school board will appoint good teachers.'

Elizabeth nodded. 'It's the same down in Sorn. They are going to extend the old school to make it bigger for all children who will now have to go. But there will be lots of children up in the hills who will not be able to get to the school in a day. I am not sure how the boards are going to see to those wains.'

'John was telling me that there is talk of the teachers going out to the hills to do some teaching in the farmhouses.'

'That will be expensive for the board,' Elizabeth said. 'I can see some ratepayers not being happy about the extra expense.'

'Hugh has got himself a good job at the local school down in Sanquhar, hasn't he? It just goes to show why getting some good larnin' is important.' Hugh was Tom and John's younger brother, who had stayed on at school and eventually trained and graduated as a teacher.

'Well, our laird says the same thing, Flora,' Elizabeth said. 'He is a good laird and is keen for his tenants to learn new methods. A couple of years ago he brought this English woman, Miss Harding is her name, to teach the womenfolk on the estate how to make Cheddar cheese.'

'Cheddar cheese!' exclaimed Flora. 'What's wrong with our Dunlop cheese?'

'Aye, well, there were plenty saying the same thing. But he's set up a good dairy business over there at Castle and he takes plenty of milk, cream and cheese off to Glasgae every day by train, so he must know his business.'

'So are the dairy maids around here making Cheddar cheese, then?' asked Flora.

'Aye, there's a fair few.'

Flora paused and considered the news that she had just heard. Could this be a way forward for the dairy at Garclaugh? She would mention it to John on the way home.

*

Once the milking and the other dairy work was finished, John, Flora and the children made their farewells and climbed into the carriage, so that Tom could take them back to the station. John had enjoyed his visit back to South Blairkip, but now he was keen to get back to his own farm.

Tom decided to take the longer road through Catrine, so that they could see the cotton mills and all the wagons loaded with bales that had fascinated them at the station. As they approached Catrine, John and Flora became aware of the noise that arose from the town. It started as a rumble, then this was interspersed with sharp bangs. Eventually they could make out the individual shouts of men, the clatter of tools and finally the source of the rumble, which was the noise from wagons being pulled along the streets and their iron-rimmed wheels rolling over the cobbles. The second sensation was the smell, which Flora said made her nose tingle. Thomas put his fingers over his nose and complained of the smell, as it reminded him of the dung heaps on the farm. Tom told them that the smell was coming from the bleaching works where the cotton cloth was soaked in lime and potash in order to give it its whiteness.

They came alongside the main mill, where the rhythmic rattle of many dozens of looms added to the cacophony of sounds. Cotton loom dust drifted in the air like fine snow, tickling their noses. The road took them around to the front of the mill where the five-storey building, with its impressive Georgian entrance, was topped by a cupola that held a large bell.

'That old bell has been ringing out for nearly a hundred years now,' Tom told them. 'In the morning the workers dread its tolling when it calls them to work and in the evening they eagerly listen for the ring that lets them go home.'

'Lots of customers for your milk and cheese, then, Tom,' John noted with a chuckle. 'I don't suppose that you are complaining too much if they bring in more workers.'

'I don't mind them bringing in more workers, so long as they keep them fully employed. When they were suffering from a lack of cotton with the American civil war, they laid off many workers who then ended up begging and stealing food from the farms,' Tom complained. 'Do you know that Uncle Hugh worked at the mills?' he added after a pause.

'Did he?' John asked. 'I thought he had a grocery business in Catrine.'

'He dinnae have a business; he just worked for a grocer. Naw, he gave that up as there was better money in the mills, although he was only a watchman. I believe some of our cousins work in the mills now, certainly the older ones Agnes, Tom and William.'

'I havnae seen them for a long time. I dinnae ken if I would recognise them if I bumped into them in the street.'

They were soon leaving the noise and bustle of Catrine and heading back up to Mauchline, where they were due to get the train back to New Cumnock. The road was busy with wagons carrying bales of raw cotton, finished boxes of white cotton cloth and all the materials and provisions needed by a thriving cotton town.

John thought about how the county had changed since his father's day, when farmers were at the whim of the laird and feeding the family was the main priority. Now, with the growth of industry in the towns and cities, the demand for the produce from farms meant that farmers had extra money to educate their families, as well as feed them, and to improve their lives. John felt good about the future for his family.

CHAPTER ELEVEN

March 1877

Flora gripped the edge of the sink as she felt the muscles tense around her abdomen. She leaned forward towards the window of the kitchen, her breath condensing on the cold glass and then trickling downwards to pool along the peeling paint at the bottom of the frame. As she waited for the contraction to ease she looked out through the misted glass across the farmyard, now quiet after the busy morning activities. She saw a forkload of wet straw come flying out of one of the shed doors and land on the growing, steaming pile of manure that was being shifted from a calf pen. A couple of hens squabbled over some grains of corn that lay in the mud, close to the house.

She straightened up as the muscles relaxed and shifted her hands to cradle and massage her enlarged abdomen. She recognised these early signs of birth as this would be her fourth child, but they had come earlier than she had expected. She had felt some tightness when she was getting dressed, but had put it down to the efforts that she had had to put into chopping up turnips during the previous day. But this was more than tightness and she would need to send for the midwife.

She continued with her task of washing the potatoes for the evening meal, although it had become increasingly difficult for Flora to work at the sink as the pregnancy progressed. She should have asked Janet, the housemaid, to do these chores, but Janet was busy around the house doing jobs that Flora could not do in her condition. At least preparing food for the meal did not involve too much bending or squatting.

Flora had washed and chopped the potatoes, and had just started on the onions, when another contraction started. This was stronger and Flora decided that this baby was now on its way and there seemed little point in waiting any longer. If it turned out to be a false alarm then Mrs McLatchie, the midwife, would just have to stay overnight.

'Janet! Janet!' she shouted from where she was standing in the kitchen. But only silence responded. Flora shuffled to the bottom of the stairs and shouted again, but there was no sound from the bedrooms. Flora was sure that she had heard Janet go upstairs earlier to put away the newly ironed sheets. She continued through to the living room where Nettie, the other maid, was with Andrew, Flora and John's second-born son.

'Have you seen Janet?' Flora asked Nettie, who was helping Andrew put together a wooden jigsaw puzzle.

'Not for a while, Mrs Baird,' replied Nettie. 'I think she might have gone outside with Mary to fetch some eggs.'

'Go and fetch her in, Nettie, I need her to go for the howdie.'

'Oh dear! Mrs Baird! Is the bairn coming?' squeaked Nettie, jumping up from the carpet.

'Aye, I think he is on his way,' Flora replied, smiling at the look of panic on Nettie's face. 'Just go and find Janet and Mary, whilst I will keep an eye on Andrew.'

Nettie ran down the corridor to the back place to find her boots. Nettie had been taken on by John and Flora in anticipation of the arrival of the new baby. She was only fourteen, but Flora knew her mother through the church and was happy to give her some work. She shared a room with Janet at the top of the farmhouse, where they could both be at hand to help around the house. Janet, who was only two years older than Nettie, had been the housemaid for a little over a year, having replaced Jessie Hamilton, who had left to get married.

There was a wail from the floor. Andrew was getting cross because he could not fit the puzzle together. Flora knelt down to help him, just as the back door to the kitchen was flung open and the two maids rushed down the corridor towards the living room.

'Oh, Mrs Baird, the bairn's coming!' Janet panted in the doorway.

Both the girls were in a flap, so, to calm them, Flora immediately issued their orders.

'Janet, you are going to have to run into town to fetch Mrs McLatchie, the howdie. You should meet Sarah on her way back with the horse and cart; she can give you a lift back into Pathhead. Mr Baird is down in the fields by the river, so you will need to get a message sent down to him. Nettie, you look after Andrew and Mary. I need to get myself sorted in case this bairn decides to come even quicker.' Flora heaved herself up using the side of the armchair. 'And where's Tom?'

'I think he is with Archie in the byre, Mrs Baird,' replied Nettie.

'Well, Janet, send Tom down with the message for his father,' Flora ordered.

Nettie knew that Tom would not be happy about having to run the chore, but, under the circumstances, there was no discussion to be had. She had only worked at the farm since the start of February but had quickly learned that you did not question an order from Mrs Baird.

Archie Wilson was the ploughman and worked around the farm on all the various jobs, but his most important role was caring for the Clydesdale horses. There were other workers who were employed at busy times of the year, but Archie was the main worker and John was keen to keep him at the farm for at least another year. Archie heard the footsteps coming towards the byre and the heavy breaths of Janet as she ran across the yard.

'Aye up, Tom, it looks as if there is trouble coming,' he said with a laugh to the small boy next to him, who was struggling to lift a heavy fork of muck from the calf pen floor.

'Tom! Tom!' panted Janet as she appeared at the door of the calf pen. 'Your mither's bairn is coming, so you need to run down and tell yer fither that we are sending for the howdie.'

Tom stood staring at Janet, taking in all that he had just been told.

'Away you go then, Tom,' said Archie. 'You need to do what your mither tells ye. You will find your faither in the field by the railway track.'

Tom gave the fork that he was using to Archie and retrieved the coat that he had hung over the door, then he ran out across the yard and into the field. Archie was quite pleased that Tom would be out of the way. Although he liked Tom, he was starting to feel like a nursemaid for the boy, because Tom would want to help Archie whenever he was trying to do a job.

Back in the house, Flora was trying to get the place in order for the arrival of the midwife and the baby. She had put the vegetables ready for the evening meal and added some more coal to the range. They would certainly need hot water before the day was out.

'Where's Mary?' she asked Nettie.

'She must still be outside with the hens,' replied Nettie.

Flora went through to the back room where a door led out into the garden. There was a blast of cold air as the door opened to give a wider view of the garden, with the hen coop at the end of the vegetable plot. Standing on the path, a few steps from the door, was Mary with eggs clutched to her chest; too many eggs. A couple of the eggs looked destined to hit the stone slabs on the path at any moment. Mary had a satisfied smile on her face.

'I collected the eggs for you, Mammy,' Mary explained proudly.

'Now you stand still, Mary, whilst I just help you with those eggs,' Flora gently said to Mary, as she moved towards her to rescue the eggs, marvelling at how she had managed to carry so many to the house without dropping any. 'You have been a grand help. Nettie, will you go into the kitchen and fetch the basket for these eggs before Mary drops them?'

Flora then leaned forward and grasped the bottom of Mary's dress, lifting it upwards to form an apron to support the eggs. 'There you are, Mary. Just open your arms and the eggs will roll into your dress.'

Mary did as she was told and the six eggs safely rolled into the apron, forming a clutch that any broody hen would have been proud to sit on. Flora hung on until Nettie was able to bring a basket and they both gently slid the eggs to safety. They both sighed with relief and Flora leaned forward to Mary, as Nettie took the eggs indoors. 'Now, that was very helpful, Mary, but you need to put the eggs carefully into a basket next time.'

'But, Mammy, Janet took the basket when Nettie fetched her,' explained Mary.

Flora realised that everyone was getting rather flustered with this baby arriving. It was time to get things settled down.

'Now, you come in and take off your boots. You can go into the living room with Nettie and play with Andrew,' Flora told Mary, as she closed the back door and Nettie reappeared from the kitchen to help Mary out of her coat.

*

Janet had set off on her journey into town. Although she was quite a small girl, she prided herself on being a good runner, even in her bulky dress and outdoor clothes, but it would still be a long run. As she ran up the track towards the main road to New Cumnock she skipped over the puddles, being careful not to get too much mud on her boots. The track into the village had recently had its puddles filled with gravel, so there was less mud to avoid.

The road into New Cumnock was straight and was bordered by a strip of trees on the southern side and fields on its northern side. Although the road mainly served the farms, it was used to transport lime from the several quarries in the area. Janet met one of these horse-drawn carts and waved at the driver.

'Hello there, lassie. You look in a hurry,' the driver shouted to her.

'Aye, I'm fetching the howdie. There's a bairn on the way,' Janet panted in reply.

As she ran past Mansfield House with its imposing gates, her footsteps echoed from the tall trees around the driveway. A guard dog barked, causing the rooks in the tops of the trees to fly up in alarm, their raucous caws adding to the discord. The dog and the sudden flight of the rooks startled Janet and made her hurry on towards the bridge over the burn. When she reached the bridge she paused for breath and leaned against the side, watching the water race on its journey to join the Nith further down the slope.

As Janet looked further along the road she could see a horse and cart coming her way. As the distance between her and the cart got smaller she was able to make out that it was Sarah, the dairy maid from the farm. Sarah had been delivering cheese to a grocery in town and was on her way back. Sarah had been working for the Bairds for four years and was now a skilled and experienced dairy maid.

Janet waited for the cart to get to her, before explaining the reason for her dash along the road. Once Janet had got herself in the cart, Sarah took it on to the entrance to Mansfield Hall, where she could turn it around for the journey back to the village to collect Mrs McLatchie.

Sarah Campbell lived with her mother and brother in a cottage on the edge of New Cumnock, in the Pathhead area. Her mother worked as a maid in Mansfield Hall and her brother worked at the Pathhead colliery. Her sister was married and lived in Kilmarnock, where she had three children. Sarah's mother often chided Sarah that she should be married as well, but Sarah always laughed and told her that she had not found a man who she respected enough to marry. The truth was probably more that Sarah's skin, particularly her face, was pitted with the scars of a cowpox infection that she had acquired when she had first started to work as a dairy maid. Cowpox was a virus that was closely related to smallpox, and it had its advantages, as it was known that dairy maids who had suffered from cowpox did not catch smallpox. However, Sarah was very conscious of her appearance and her pox marks. She had heard the comments that some thoughtless people made behind her back and had even had to suffer jibes from cruel youngsters who shouted 'pox face' at her as she passed.

Mrs McLatchie lived in one of the cottages in Pathhead, close to Sarah's home. Sarah had spoken to her that morning as she had left with her mother to go to work, so she knew that she would be at home. In fact, when they had spoken, Mrs McLatchie had asked after Flora's health and the state of the baby, but at that time Sarah had no news. As Sarah knocked at Mrs McLatchie's door, Janet made herself as comfortable as possible in the back of the cart, next to the empty cheese boxes. Mrs McLatchie kept all her midwifery bits in a bag that she could pick up quickly, so she was soon sitting on the cart seat next to Sarah on her way to the farm.

Like many howdies or midwives, Cath McLatchie started her work in search of income after the death of her husband, who was killed working on the new railway line. Although the medical authorities were trying to introduce more training for midwives, most midwives learned 'on the job' by watching and helping more experienced midwives. Cath had never been properly trained and had a low opinion of doctors and their ability to supervise a birthing. One of the local doctors had told her that she was too old to be a midwife and that she needed to give it up for younger, properly trained midwives. Cath was seventy-three; she considered herself as sprightly as a woman half her age, and had twice as much experience.

As they travelled back down Mansfield Road they could see a mist rolling down over Craigdullyeart Hill to the north. What weak sunshine had broken through the thin clouds had long since vanished, but at least the clouds did not look full of rain. It was a typical early March day, with the promise of warmer days to come, but with the reality that there was still plenty of time for frosts and even snow.

There was little chatter between the three travellers. Cath McLatchie seemed content to doze by Sarah, who made no effort to talk to her or to Janet. Janet had found it hard work talking to Sarah, who usually only replied to her attempts at conversation with a few words or sometimes just a grunt. But Janet had watched Sarah when she was working in the dairy and had always been impressed by her skills. She had realised that she could learn a lot from watching Sarah and she knew that a skilled dairy maid was a valued person in the Ayrshire farming community.

In the end Janet could not tolerate the silence any longer.

'So, Mrs McLatchie,' she said over her shoulder to Cath McLatchie's back. 'Did you deliver the other bairns for Mrs Baird?'

Cath jerked awake with a small cry. 'What? What was that ye said?'

Janet repeated her question.

'Och aye. Not the first yen, but the other twa. What are their names?' she asked as she trawled her memory. But, before Janet could reply, she continued. 'She was new over here. Came from Auchinleck, I seem to recall, so she called on a howdie that her family had used.'

'The older boy is Tom. So you must have delivered Mary and Andrew,' Janet told her.

'Aye. A lassie, then a laddie. Both healthy and bonnie,' Cath replied, her voice trailing off absent-mindedly.

They arrived at Mansfield, along with the mist. The caws from the rooks seemed to make the mist even more threatening, as did the barking of the dog at Mansfield House. Janet shivered and wished that she had brought her shawl. But it was only a short distance to the entrance to Meikle Garclaugh, so she would soon be able to warm herself by the fire. Although, with Mrs Baird going into labour, she doubted whether she would have the time; perhaps she would have to warm herself working through the many jobs that she knew she would be given.

As the horse and cart pulled into the yard, Archie came out of the sheds to hold the harness and steady the horse. The three women climbed down and Archie led the horse and cart away to unhitch the cart and remove the tackle, so that he could give the horse a wipe down.

John Baird had returned from the fields and was now standing in front of the door.

'You are welcome, Mrs McLatchie,' he announced in his usual loud cheery voice. 'Come on in and warm yourself. Mrs Baird has only just gone upstairs, so there's no panic just yet.'

'I don't panic, Mr Baird,' Cath responded, mildly affronted.

John laughed. 'Well, you will be the only one, because everyone else seems to be in a panic.'

As Cath McLatchie made her way into the kitchen to warm herself by the range, John turned to Janet and gave her some instructions that Flora had been very particular that he should pass on. Janet listened, then hurried around to the back door to remove her boots and get on with the jobs with which Mrs Baird had charged her. Sarah also turned and walked over to the dairy to get on with another batch of cheeses. The jobs in the house and on the farm would continue, despite the imminent arrival of another Baird bairn.

*

Dr Richard Robertson came by during the next morning, having received a note from John that the new baby had arrived. The baby boy had arrived in the evening of the 2nd March and as the third son, in the Scottish tradition, was named after his father, John. He was also given the middle name James, as both John and Flora had brothers called James.

Richard gave the baby a thorough examination and pronounced him healthy. Like all mothers, Flora's first concern was that the baby would be normal. A disabled baby would be a drain on the family. Midwives often left the umbilical cord untied if the baby had an obvious disability, and the baby would bleed to death and be recorded as stillborn.

'How's Margo, Richard?' Flora asked, knowing that Margo was also in the latter stages of a pregnancy.

'Oh, she's fine, thank you for asking, Flora,' Richard replied, as he checked Flora's temperature and abdomen. 'We, of course, are looking forward to our own little boy.'

Flora laughed. 'She's certain that this one's a boy, then?'

'Well, she says that it feels different and it is kicking her far harder than the other two ever did.' He paused, his mind going back to medical matters. 'Has the howdie checked that the afterbirth was intact, Flora?'

'Aye, she's showed me it as well for me to check. It was all there,' Flora replied.

Richard knew that over the next few days it would be important to monitor Flora to ensure that she did not fever and that there was no bleeding. Far too many mothers died within weeks of childbirth due to infections. Thankfully Flora was an experienced mother, so he was not too concerned about any problems. He finished his checks of Flora and watched as wee John snuggled into his mother's breast for a feed.

'He certainly has an appetite,' he chuckled, packing his bag. 'I'll leave you twa in peace.'

When Richard reached the kitchen, John had returned from giving the cows their feed of chopped turnips and was warming himself by the range.

'All well upstairs, then, Richard?' he enquired.

'Aye, all well. One very healthy baby and one healthy mother.'

'Thank you very much for coming over. I know that you must be busy in town with the measles outbreak.'

'Aye, we are, and it doesn't look like abating,' Richard said. 'We have been considering asking to close the schools for a week or so to try and halt the spread. But we have to wait for the school boards to meet and decide, which could take a few days. In the meantime there are more children coming down with it. We have had a couple of deaths over in the miners' rows. After the long winter the wains just don't have much strength to fight off the fever.'

John nodded. 'We have kept Tom away from school for the last two days, as it seems that many of his class have gone down with it. If we didn't have the bairn due, we would have let him get the measles and be done with it.'

'Well, you won't be the only parents thinking that. Most children get over the measles without a problem, but it can bring on other problems like deafness and lung infections, which is what caused the deaths of the miners' children. Their homes are so damp that many of the children have lung infections anyway, even before they pick up measles.'

'With the price of bread having gone up as well, there will be many of the poor folk struggling to feed their wains properly,' John said. 'We could do with a good summer and a good harvest this year. After three wet summers, we must surely be due a good year?'

'It's all down to the good Lord, John, as you know.' Richard took up his coat and riding crop as he made his way through the back room to the door out into the yard. His horse was tied up by the byre and Archie had given him a bag of hay. He led his horse over to the mounting block that was set into the wall of the byre. He used it to climb into the saddle, and John bade him a safe journey back into town.

As Richard rode out of the yard, John saw a couple of figures walking down the farm track. It was Grace Houston, his neighbour, and her oldest daughter Mary. He waited in the yard for their arrival.

'Good marnin', John,' Grace greeted John. 'I hear that the baby has arrived safely.'

John laughed. 'Bye, news travels quickly around here. He's only been in this world for just over half a day!'

'Well, Mrs McLatchie likes to announce her successful deliveries to the whole community, if she can.'

'Come on in, you two. I'll ask Flora if she is up for visitors.'

Grace and Mary were soon upstairs cooing over the new baby in the main bedroom. Wee John's little sister Mary had also joined the group. After a while they came downstairs to the kitchen, where John had got Janet to warm up some whey for the visitors.

Whilst the two Marys were talking, Grace chose a moment to speak to John. 'My Andrew asked me to ask you if you had had any further thoughts about speaking to the factor about the rents.'

'Aye, Grace, I have. Tell your husband that if he wants to come over this afternoon I thought that we could go over to see the factor together. I was hoping that Will Gilmour and Jack Picken would join us, but they say that they don't want to cause any problem with Lady Jane,' John replied.

'That's fine. I will tell him,' Grace said. 'We've been really struggling this last year since losing our dairy maid. We haven't been able to get a good replacement and I can't manage all the work with the wains to look after.' She paused. 'I'm sorry, John, you don't want to hear aboot oor troubles. I hope that the factor will do the decent thing and speak to

Lady Jane, but if he does it will be the first time that he has done something decent.' She rose from the chair and called for her daughter. 'Thanks very much, John. You're a good neighbour and we are grateful for yer help.'

John stood at the back door and watched them walk away, up the farm track back to their home. He had hoped that Andrew Houston would be able to make a better job of farming Wee Garclaugh, after his cousin's poor efforts. With six children under ten years old, the Houstons really needed to get the farm earning money.

*

Later that day Andrew Houston came over to Meikle Garclaugh and met up with John. The two farmers walked down the road to Mansfield House, where they had arranged to meet with Samuel Adam, the factor for the Mansfield estate. The laird who had taken over after the death of Sir James Stuart Menteath was an absent laird and spent most of his time in New York. His aunt, Sir James's widow, looked after the two estates in his absence. However, she relied heavily on her factor, Samuel Adam, who had managed the estate at Mansfield for over twenty-five years. He was an old man now and had not mellowed in his old age. Few people in the community had a good word to say for him.

The door to the factor's office, which was to the side of the main house, was opened by the coachman, Jack Wilkie.

'Good day, Mr Baird and Mr Houston,' Jack greeted them.

'Good day to you, Jack. I hope that yer family are all well?' John asked.

But before Jack could reply a voice came from the office. 'Just show them through, Wilkie.'

Jack raised his eyebrows at the two farmers and ushered them through to the office.

'So, Mr Baird, Mr Houston. What can I do for you? I expect you have come to ask for the rents to be lowered?' Samuel Adam greeted them.

'And a guid afternoon to you, Mr Adam,' John replied, taking a seat on one of the chairs in front of a large desk. The office was a reasonably large room, but it was made smaller by the intrusion of a variety of wooden cupboards, shelves and piles of legal papers, tied up with ribbon. It was very clear that this was where the estate was managed and it was very clear that Samuel Adam was at its centre.

John continued. 'Aye, well, since ye have raised the topic then you will ken why we are asking. We are asking for the rents to be deferred for three months. Ye ken we have had three bad harvests and the price of feed grain has risen to as high as I can remember. We are not getting the income that we were getting just three years ago. With the longer winters we have had to use savings to buy in extra fodder. We just need a good harvest and to get the coos out on the grass early and we will be able to pay the rent without problem.' He paused and waited for a response.

'It's out of the question,' the factor replied. 'The estate has had rising costs as well, and we have also had a falling income over the past three years. You will just have to use more of yer savings to get through to the summer and then pray for a good harvest. Now is there anything else?' He stared at the two farming neighbours in turn.

John answered. 'Aye, there is. The two meadows by the railway line need draining properly. We dug some sheughs four years ago, but they have filled with clay washed down from the hill. What it needs is some proper pipes and a full ditch dug next to the railway line. I am asking if the estate would pay for this improvement work to be done.'

The factor leaned back in his chair and there was a creaking sound that could have been the chair or the ancient joints of Samuel Adam himself. 'I'll discuss it with Lady Menteath when I meet with her next. I will let you know her reply.' He leaned forward and picked up some papers from his desk, showing that the meeting had finished. 'Wylie! Please show Mr Baird and Mr Houston oot.'

The two men looked at each other with a certain amount of resignation. John had not expected much to come out of the meeting and had only really agreed to go to the factor in order to support his neighbour. He rose from his chair and they left the office. On their way out, Wylie congratulated John on the birth of his baby son.

'Well, that was a short meeting,' Andrew said to John as they walked up the driveway of the big house.

'Aye. I wasn't expecting much, but the least he could have done was offer to speak to Lady Jane for us. The old laird would have had the decency to meet with us himself. It seems that Mr Adam fancies himself as the new laird.'

The two men walked on in silence. After a while John turned to his neighbour. 'This new girl that you have working for ye. What's her name?'

'Isabella,' Andrew replied.

'Send her over to the dairy some time and I'll get Sarah to teach her some of her cheese-making skills. At least we can get you back into cheese production again. It will help add to yer milk income. We then just have to pray that we get an early spring and can get these coos out in the fields before we run out of feed.'

'Yer a good man, John Baird. I'll send her up tomorrow morning, when we get back from taking the milk to the station.'

As the two men walked back to Garclaugh they talked of the new Ayrshire Cattle Society that was being formed. They were both pleased that the breed in which they had such pride had at last been recognised with its own society. The society would be able to record the bloodlines of top Ayrshire cattle and distribute information about top herds and prize-winning cows and bulls. Both men hoped that they would be able to profit by breeding top-quality cattle. At least this was something hopeful in these times of high prices and low incomes.

CHAPTER TWELVE
June 1873

James Stevenson was taking a gamble; he knew it. He was moving his young family across the country, in fact to a different country, to take up the tenancy of a farm in the Nith valley. He was a good farmer and had turned Eels Farm in Northumberland into a profitable concern, despite the downturn in agriculture over the past few years. Now he wanted to work for himself, not make profits for an absent employer.

James and his family were waiting at Hexham station for the train from Newcastle to arrive, onto which would be loaded all their possessions. He would have liked to have loaded some of the dairy cows that he had bred over the previous ten years, but as he had been a farm manager, rather than a tenant, the cattle belonged to his employer.

James had been born into farming at Lady Yard Farm at Tarbolton, not so far away from New Cumnock. The Stevenson family were well known in the area as dairy farmers. James, however, had moved to England to manage a farm near Hexham, where his young family had been born and had grown, along with his desire to return to Ayrshire. His brother had told him about a farm near New Cumnock, owned by the Marquis of Bute, whose lease was now available. James had travelled over to meet the factor and discuss taking on the lease, and he had been accepted. Nether Cairn was a large farm of 500 acres that looked down from the hillside on the River Nith, not unlike Meikle Garclaugh. The difference was that Nether Cairn was situated to the south of the river and was further downstream, next to the road to Kirkconnel. It was mainly good land and James considered himself fortunate to have the opportunity to farm it and for his family to become part of the local community.

'How's the bairn?' James asked his wife, more to break his nervousness than to genuinely enquire.

'She's fine. Although I may have to use the cloakroom to change her nappy afore we get on the train or she'll be mingin,' Annie replied, cradling baby Barbara.

James looked around for his two elder sons James and Allan. They were at the end of the platform, watching a shunting engine moving wagons around in one of the sidings. John, his third son, was sitting at the end of the bench, whilst his daughters Jessie and Annie were playing with their dollies next to his wife.

'I'll look after the wains, if you want to go now. The train is due in fairly soon, although it will take them a while to load all our crates and bags.' He sat between the two older girls and John, pleased to take his mind off the journey ahead. They would not get to Carlisle until after noon and they then had to catch the Glasgow and South Western train to Kirkconnel. It would mean having to transfer all their baggage from one part of the station to another.

'When are we going home, Paw?' John asked his father.

'We won't be going back to the farm, John. We are going to move to a new farm in Scotland, near to where Grannie lives.'

John swung his legs underneath the bench and stared at the ground. 'Will my friend Jamie be able to visit?'

'I'm not sure if Jamie's maw and paw will be able to take him. It is a lang distance from oor auld farm to the new yen.' James tried to console his youngest son. 'You'll be able to make some new friends.'

There was a clatter of boots down the platform. 'The train's here, Paw!' his eldest son shouted.

James looked down the tracks to see the white plumes of steam drifting across the roofs of the houses that lined the trackside. Behind him the station started to bustle into life and James turned to see the station master walk out of his office and then pull a shiny silver watch from his waistcoat pocket. The station master pressed a catch on the side of the watch and the cover sprang open to reveal the dial, which he studied for a few seconds before closing the cover and returning the watch to his pocket with a satisfied grunt. The train had clearly met the high standards of punctuality demanded on Victorian railways.

There was no sign of his wife Annie, so James collected his children around him and reminded the older boys of which bags they need to carry into the carriage. The train slowed into the platform and passed in front of them, giving off a smell of hot oil and soot. The brakes squealed on and the carriages rattled and banged to a stop, making little Annie, who was only two years old, clung to her father's trousers. 'I don't like it,' she protested. James picked her up and she clung around his neck, hiding her face from the fearsome machine that had suddenly invaded her quiet time on the platform with her sister.

'Don't fret, wee Annie. I'll keep you safe,' he soothed her.

The howl of a crying baby projected into the noises on the platform and Barbara, the source of the crying, appeared from the cloakroom in her mother's arms. Annie called over her eldest son. 'Here, James, take the bairn.' She lifted Barbara towards the boy, who looked in disgust at his mother, but before he could register his protest the baby was dumped into his arms. He struggled to get a good grip as his little sister squirmed around. She might only be a year old, but she was strong and knew what she liked and disliked. Being in the arms of someone who was not her mother was definitely a dislike.

The family started to get their bags sorted and one of the platform staff helped them find the carriage that they had booked. Once the younger children were all seated in the carriage, James went back onto the platform to check that the mound of boxes containing their possessions was being loaded into one of the goods wagons at the back of the train.

'Don't worry, Mr Stevenson,' James heard the station master say behind him. 'They'll get all your boxes loaded without a problem. I have telegraphed Carlisle to make sure that they have enough porters on hand to help you unload and get your connection up to Kirkconnel.'

James thanked the station master, then joined his family in the carriage. 'Well, that's done, then. We leave one life behind us and enter a new life in Scotland,' he announced with a broad grin.

His children looked back at him with less convinced expressions, the novelty and excitement of a train journey having faded to a realisation that they were leaving their home and their friends behind.

'Will I have to share a room with Allan and John again?' asked wee James.

James's grin faded and his own nervousness crept back to him. Was this a rash move? He had saved a fair bit of money in the bank to help him get started as a tenant farmer, but would it get him through the first few years when he knew that the farm would not be earning much income?

'Yes, you will have to share a room. In fact you will be sharing a room until the day that you are old enough to go oot and find your own hoose.' James silenced his son with a stare.

James settled back into his seat and pondered on the move that he was making with his family. He was filled with both excitement and trepidation, but was confident that this was the right change to make in their lives.

CHAPTER THIRTEEN

July 1878

It wasn't a large elephant, but it was the biggest animal that young Tom Baird had ever seen. After all the squeals of excitement in the playground when they had been let out of their classrooms by the headmaster, the children stood in near silence as animals that they had only ever seen described in books came along the road past their school. The elephant had a multi-coloured cloth hanging over its back and a sparkling triangle of cloth on its forehead. Tom was transfixed by its image as soon as it appeared on the road. It swayed from side to side as it walked between the crowds on both sides of the road, its keeper prodding it with a long stick and talking to it quietly in order to keep it calm.

'That elephant has a nose as big as your paw's nose, Tom,' a squeaky giggling voice said behind Tom, to a chorus of other giggles.

Tom turned to face the boy who had made the comment. 'And it has a stomach as big as your mither's, George Sloan,' he replied to his tormentor's face, to yet more giggles from the crowd of boys that stood around the pair.

The two boys grabbed hold of each other and the other children surrounded them, hoping to see a fine scrap. However, a large hand took each boy by the collar and held them apart.

'I tak it that you twa dinnae want to watch any more of the circus?' said Mr Nairn, the headmaster.

'Aye, sir. I mean no, Mr Nairn. Sorry, sir,' Tom spluttered, followed by a similar apology from George. The two boys stared at each other, each knowing that this scrap was only postponed, not cancelled.

*

Opposite the school, Dr Richard Robertson had left the surgery with Margo and two of his four daughters. He too was marvelling at the various animals that formed part of Wombwell's Menagerie. They were passing through New Cumnock on the way up to Glasgow, but were stopping at towns in order to feed and rest the animals and to earn some money from their shows. The menagerie had planned to stop at Old Cumnock for the night, but the large traction engine pulling a wagon loaded with tents, long poles and other heavy equipment had got stuck on Afton Bridge, in front of the Old Mill. It had taken them a long while to extract the machine because it meant knocking down part of the parapet of the old stone bridge. So the journey to Old Cumnock would be delayed, and it had been decided that the whole show would pitch up on Castle Green in town.

'Good afternoon, Dr Robertson,' a voice nearby greeted Richard. He turned to find Gilbert Sloan, a local grocery merchant. Richard had first met him five years previously when the water committee had been established to bring piped water into the town. Richard had been an enthusiastic committee member but had eventually resigned because of the constant indecision and wrangling about where to source the water and how to pay for the work.

'This is certainly keeping the children entertained,' Gilbert said, pointing across the road to the line of faces peering through the school fence. 'I expect my lad George will be somewhere amongst them. He wouldn't want to miss a sight like this.'

'It is keeping many people entertained,' replied Richard, pointing to the long line of local people bordering the road both down to the Old Mill and up to Castle. 'The nonsense at the bridge allowed news to spread through the toon, so many folk had time to drop what they were doing and come oot to gander.'

'Well, I've been telling the council for a lang time that the bridge is too narrow. It's hard enough trying to get a large wagon through it, let alone a great big bit of tackle like a traction engine,' Gilbert noted. 'They will have to do something now that the walls are falling doon.'

'So, you are looking well, Mr Sloan. How's your stomach these days?' Richard enquired.

'Oh, it's much better now, thank you for asking, Richard. I think it was all that fuss with the Glasgae Bank that caused it to get bad in the first place. It was a worrying time.'

Richard nodded. 'Yes, my father-in-law tells me that the bank is in good shape now and is paying 12% dividends this year. He has been trying to persuade me to buy shares, but I am happy enough to invest in the practice, rather than gamble with shares.'

'Very canny, Richard, very canny,' replied Gilbert. The two men paused in their conversation to watch some camels being led past them. 'I thought that camels had two humps?'

'I believe that there are two species of camel. One species has two humps and one has one,' Richard explained.

'And do they store water in the humps?'

'I have read that it is mainly fat, not water,' Richard replied. 'So, how is our water storage project going, Mr Sloan?'

Gilbert Sloan chuckled at Richard's clever change of the subject, although not the substance being discussed. 'Aye, it's going well. Ye will have seen that they have put in quite a lot of stand pipes in Castle, so they have nearly finished over there. They have been some issues about where the stand pipes will be placed. Some people want them further away from their properties, some others want them closer. Ye cannie please everyone. We should have it completed by the end of the year, as we planned.'

'I seem to remember that the original plan was to get it completed by the end of 1885,' Richard remarked.

'Aye, well. You were on the committee at the time and saw the issues that were slowing things doon.'

'The biggest mistake was appointing that civil engineer from Edinburgh. It was clear after the big public meeting in '76 that he had got all his figures wrong. At least there seems to be some progress cleaning up the rivers. The coal companies have agreed to dig proper cesspits for the miners' rows. Once we get the clean water to the rows, then perhaps we can see an end to the regular epidemics.'

Gilbert turned away from the passing wagons to look at Richard. 'The rows are not being connected to the water pipes.'

'What?' exclaimed Richard. 'So the miners' families are going to have to continue to take water from the polluted wells?'

'I understand that Bank Coal Company are considering taking their own supply from the hill to feed the steam engines and the rows.'

'That sounds like the coal companies: look after their machines before their workers.'

'Aye, well, that's what I've heard,' Gilbert said, rather sheepishly, realising that he had touched on a subject on which Richard had some strong and passionate views. He decided to move the discussion away from the morals of the coal companies. 'And how is the practice going? I have heard that Dr Cluny is going to be selling it to you soon.'

'Well, that's just a bit of local gossip, I'm afraid,' Richard said pointedly. 'He is spending more time over in Ayr with his son's practice, but he is still a full partner here.'

'Aye, well, ye ken how folk love to blether. There will be plenty of folk in toon would be happy to see ye tak on the whole practice.' Gilbert paused and watched the last of the menagerie wagons pass in front of them. 'Well, I'll be on my way. Good day to you, Richard, and to you, Mrs Robertson.'

Richard watched Mr Stirling, the school's second master, chiding the children back into their classrooms, as Mr Nairn stood by the school doorway. Richard's eldest daughter Jane was at the school now, and Richard was pleased with the schooling that she was receiving. Mr Nairn saw Richard watching and gave him a wave, which Richard acknowledged.

*

The menagerie caused a lot of excitement in the town, and later in the afternoon John, Flora and the family were dragged down to see the animals by a very excited Tom, who could not get out his words fast enough to tell his father about the elephant that he had seen. It grew in size as he described it, until it was large enough to block the whole road into town. But it was the lions that caused the biggest stir in the crowds that gathered on Castle Green that summer's evening. Their cages had been covered as they had travelled through the town, because many horses had bolted and some thrown their riders at the sight of the beasts. Even the smell of them caused horses to stir and stamp their feet uneasily as they passed. But down on the green the covers had been removed and the paying public could see the pair of lions prowling back and forth behind the bars of their cage. John was most impressed, although Mary clung to her father's neck. Unlike Tom, she had been very nervous at the school as she had watched the animals with the rest of her class.

As the evening drew darker the family returned home, with many interesting memories of their visit to Wombwell's Menagerie. It was a story that Tom would be able to tell his cousins when he met up with them in the future.

CHAPTER FOURTEEN
September 1878

But pleasures are like poppies spread,
You seize the flower, its bloom is shed;
Or like the snow falls in the river;
A moment white – then melts for ever.

'Tam O'Shanter', Robert Burns

Farming was still a struggle in the Nith valley. Although the previous summer had produced a good harvest, the cost of grain was still high, so for dairy farmers like the Bairds, who only grew enough oats to feed their cattle, any extra grain that was needed for winter feed was increasing their costs. However, the demand for fresh milk and cheeses continued to grow, and this gave them a steady income on which they could rely. John Baird's herd of Ayrshire cows was thriving under his expert management and he now had some good young bull calves, which he was confident would fetch good prices at a future cattle sale.

At Garclaugh, John, Flora and the family were enjoying the company of their good friends Dr Richard Robertson, his wife Margo and their four daughters. Despite Margo's confidence that her latest child was going to be a son, they would have to wait longer. The older children were running around in the orchard on this warm Sunday in late September. John and Richard were looking across the fields down to the River Nith.

'I see that there is still water lying on your river meadows, John,' Richard noted.

'Aye, well, the Lammas floods put a lot of water onto those fields. They do not drain easily; in fact some areas in the middle of the meadows are more like bogs. If you walk on them you can feel the ground bouncing on the water below. I have been trying to find some way to drain them properly, but they are so close to the level of the river that the water takes a long time to move off them. Perhaps I should accept that they will always be wet fields.' John paused for a moment. 'Someone was telling me that, a few hundred years ago, there used to be a lake at the bottom of those fields. They took out the dam of rock that was holding it back and let the water drain awa, so that it left just the river. It's not surprising that those fields are so wet, if they were at the bottom of a lake once.'

'How remarkable,' said Richard. 'So, the storms in July and August, or the Lammas rains, as you call them: they are a regular event?'

'Well, you must have seen the effects when you were living down in Dumfries. Some years the rains are barely more than a few showers, then in other years the rivers burst their banks and animals and even people drown. It is all in the hands of the Lord as to what we will get each year. I am sure that He has a plan, whatever that may be.'

'The weather down near the coast was quite different to up here in the hills. The river used to get high but rarely went over its banks by the time it got down to Dumfries,' Richard commented.

'We always plan for the Lammas floods,' John said. 'It means that we have to try and get the hay collected before the rains come, otherwise the hay ends up doon the river. This year we did not get it all in before the rains came, so we could be short of fodder. Let's hope that we have a short winter this year.'

Flora and Margo were playing with the little ones, whilst the older children were down in the orchard chasing each other and having a grand time.

'It's nice to see the wains having such fun. They do get on well together,' said Margo.

'They have grown up together; it's like they are cousins. Our laddies and your lassies,' Flora responded.

'Aye, well, perhaps one day I can add a laddie,' Margo replied sadly.

'Wheesht, it's only a matter of time, Margo. You must surely be due for a laddie for the next one.'

'If the good Lord wants us to have all girls then who are we to question his plan? But I know that Richard would so much like a son,' Margo said. 'We will continue to pray for a son.'

Their attention turned to wee John, who was struggling to walk on the grass. Mary, his six-year-old sister, was helping him walk by holding his hands. Margo's youngest daughter, only just a year old, was crawling on a rug that Margo had spread on the grass at the top of the orchard.

'Your John is coming on well, Flora. He is a happy bairn, always seems to have a smile.'

'Aye, he's growing fast.' Flora's attention was suddenly drawn to the children's play. 'Thomas!' she shouted down the orchard. 'Stop teasing Andrew and let him play with the others.' She paused and then turned to Margo. 'He can be a tiresome lad at times. I seem to have to chide him often about the way that he annoys Mary and Andrew.'

'Well, he's the oldest and he believes that he is in charge, Flora. That's the way with the eldest,' Margo said with a laugh.

'How are your parents, Margo? I haven't seen them for a while in town. I expect your faither is busy with the bank.'

'Aye, he seems very happy with the way things are going. The directors have just announced some good dividends, so the shareholders are happy. Faither has been trying to persuade Richard to buy some shares, but Richard wants to wait until the practice is sorted.'

'So what is happening with the practice?' Flora asked. 'Everyone seems to believe that Dr Cluny is going to be leaving soon.'

'Things have not been completely settled, but Richard has agreed a price with Thomas Cluny. Thomas wants to move to Ayr and work part-time with his son's practice there. We have already borrowed the money from the Glasgae bank and paid him. But this must be in confidence; Richard wouldn't want it to add to the gossip that is already around town.'

'I won't mention it to a soul, Margo,' Flora replied.

*

It was only a few days after the families had enjoyed their warm September Sunday afternoon together that the news that the Bank of Glasgow had gone bankrupt spread through the town. Traders, business people and ordinary townsfolk who had accounts with the bank rushed up to Pathhead, where the New Cumnock branch was located. A crowd had grown outside the bank doors, which were firmly closed. Pinned to the door was a notice, signed by Alex Craig, which stated that the bank had ceased trading whilst negotiations were taking place to see if the bank could be saved. No money could be withdrawn until further notice.

There was a mixture of reactions in the crowd of bank customers, from shocked silence to vocal anger. Alex Craig, Margo's father, sat in his office inside the bank. One or two of the other staff were pacing around, keeping away from the windows.

'What shall we do now, Mr Craig?' one of the clerks asked Alex.

Alex shifted in his chair and looked out at the rest of the staff, who were all looking in his direction for some guidance. He realised that there was little point in the staff sitting around with nothing to do, worrying about their own futures with no jobs.

'Tidy your desks. Fetch all the money trays and put them in the safe. Then take your coats and go home. Use the rear door to avoid the crowd. If anyone asks what is happening to their money, just tell them the truth: that you dinnae ken.'

The staff followed his instructions and left. Alex remained sitting at his desk, listening to the angry customers outside. He felt betrayed. How could the bank be in such bad shape? It was only a month ago that details of the bank's considerable holdings had been published. Why were they issuing such large dividends if the bank had no money? He would take the train up to Glasgow in the morning and find out what was happening at first hand. In the meantime he would have to walk home past neighbours and friends who had money in the bank and who now feared that it was all lost. He knew how they felt, because not only did Alex have his family's savings in the bank, but he also had shares.

He debated with himself whether he should leave by the front door or the rear door. He decided on the former. He put the last of the money trays and the account books in the safe and locked it. He then tidied his desk, took his coat and stood ready to open the front door.

As he opened it there was a sudden surge of angry voices.

'What's happening, Craig?'

'Have we lost oor money?'

'There must be money in your safe. Let us get it now.'

'Did ye ken aforehand, Craig?'

Alex raised his hand to speak and the voices quietened. 'I am very sorry, but I am as ignorant as you about what is happening. The first that I knew was when I received a telegram this morning. I am going to

Glasgae tomorrow to find oot more information and will put up a notice in the evening when I return.'

The angry voices continued, but there was now a resignation behind their tone. Some people started to walk away and the crowd of curious onlookers began to disperse. Alex again gave his apologies to individual customers and quietly asked them to go home and wait for further news. Eventually the area quietened down and the only watchers were the children who stood around looking disappointed that all the noise had not created more action for them to enjoy. Alex began the walk to his house, which would seem much longer than normal on this day.

Many years later most of the residents of New Cumnock could describe where they were and what they were doing when they heard about the Glasgow Bank going bust. Dr Richard was in his surgery when there was a frantic knocking at his door and Margo entered with apologies to the patient that Richard was examining.

'Can I speak with you, Richard, urgently?' She wore panic on her face and Richard was filled with dread as to what news she would bring. He joined Margo in the hallway.

'The Glasgae Bank has gone, Richard. What will Faither do? I must go to him.'

'What? What do you mean, the bank has gone?'

'It's gone bankrupt.'

'Bankrupt? How do ye ken?' Richard asked.

'It's all over the toon. Everyone's talking about it. Faither has put a notice on the door of the bank telling customers that they cannot withdraw any money until further notice. There are a lot of frightened and angry people up at the bank. Oh, poor Faither, Richard. What shall I do? Do I go up there?'

'Your faither will be busy in the bank. Go to your mither; she will be worried for Alex too.'

'Aye. I'll do that.' Margo turned and walked away briskly to get the maid to look after the children, leaving Richard to watch her retreating back and absorb what he had just been told. His patient was curious about the interruptions, so Richard told her the news.

'It's all over toon, so it's not as if I am telling you a secret,' he reasoned.

Later that afternoon Margo returned to tell Richard what she knew and described the fragile state of her father after he returned from the bank.

'Oh, Richard, you should have seen him. He just came in and sank into his chair. He sat there for a lang time without a word, just staring at the grate. Mither and I didn't know what to say or do. Eventually he got up and went to his desk and started sifting through his papers. He's going up to Glasgae tomorrow to find oot more about the future. Faither has all the family's money in the bank, Richard. How much do we have in the bank?'

'We don't have a lot in the main account, because I have just paid off some of the loan.' He paused. 'I wonder what will happen to the loan. Will I still have to repay it? If the bank is no longer trading, then to whom do I repay it?'

Alex Craig's trip to Glasgow proved fruitless. All the doors to the headquarters were closed and the police were on hand to control a huge crowd of angry customers who were filling the street. There was no news being released that indicated that the bank was going to be rescued; in fact the only news that trickled out was how much the bank was in debt. The figures were huge; they owed millions of pounds, having told investors only a few months previously that they had healthy assets of millions of pounds.

Over the next few weeks, traders and businesses began to close and their families packed their bags into carts and left their homes as they had no money to pay rents. In New Cumnock a number of businesses closed and the community rallied around to help the families who were now destitute. Alex Craig almost became a recluse as angry Bank of Glasgow customers vented their frustration at him. Fortunately there were enough sensible people in the town who realised that Alex was as much a victim as other folk. Eventually he could venture out in the street without remarks being shouted across at him and children chanting cruel names.

Richard Robertson soon realised that there would be a group of customers who would benefit from the bank's collapse and he would be one of them. As he had wondered many weeks before, there was now no bank to which he had to repay the money he had borrowed, so he now owned his practice outright and was not burdened with a loan. It's an ill wind that blows nobody good.

*

At the end of November, a cold wind began to blow from the north. An early winter snow gave the hills white tops, but soon the snow crept further down their slopes until it pitched in the valley. As November drifted into December, so did the snow. It continued to fall, blown by a bitterly cold wind, into drifts along the hedgerows.

John had had a good turnip crop, so he had a good supply of fodder for the cattle. He was not unduly worried as the frost turned the soil into the hardness of rock. The potatoes and turnips were covered with a thick layer of straw to protect them from the frost, which would otherwise cause them to rot once a thaw set in.

Soon after the turn of the year the water board advertised the grand opening of the water system. The opening would have been more successful if many of the pipes had not been frozen solid. Where water pipes were exposed, as they ran under the bridges or across ditches, the newly appointed 'water engineer' tried unsuccessfully to unfreeze the pipes by building fires under them. Pathhead and Mansfield were without water for nearly two months, until the temperatures rose enough to allow a natural thaw. Fortunately, the Blubber Well at Garclaugh continue to produce a steady flow of water, even during the coldest days when the temperatures dropped to many degrees below freezing point, so the farm always had access to water for the cattle and for washing the dairy.

Cart in turnip field.
Courtesy of Terry Harrison

As Hogmanay had approached, most people had looked forward to a new year when they could put behind them the troubles and problems of the past year and welcome the promises of a better year. Like all farmers, John Baird had wished for the end of winter and for a year of good weather, whilst Flora just hoped for her children to remain healthy. Margo Robertson was pregnant again and she prayed that the new baby would be the son for which her husband yearned.

The cold weather and the deep snow continued through January and into February. By March, all the farms were hunting for fodder. Some had even chosen to send some of their older milk cows for slaughter, in order to reduce the demand for food for the cattle. Poor straw, which would normally be kept for bedding, was now being mixed with the last of the hay.

John was standing looking at his herd when Robert Burnett, their new ploughman and general farmhand, approached.

'They're looking cold and hungry,' Robert commented, not that John needed it pointed out to him.

'If this winter doesn't end soon, they are going to get hungrier still,' John replied. 'We'll thresh the last of the oats this week, which will give the horses some more feed and the cattle some more straw. I'm going to have to buy in some more mash from the brewers in toon to try and keep them fed until we can get them outside in the fields.'

'I've heard that the brewers are charging twice their normal price for mash,' Robert said.

'Aye, you can always rely on someone making money from the misery of others.'

Breweries and distilleries malted barley to make their ales and whiskies. Once the malted barley had been fermented and the alcohol separated, the mash that was left over could still be eaten by animals, although it lacked much of the sugars that would provide sustenance. Farmers mixed the mash with other crops, like turnips, to provide their animals with a proper feed.

John stamped his feet to warm them. 'Well, standing around looking at them is nae going to mak them any less hungry or warmer.'

'I wanted to ask you, Mr Baird, whether ye would mind if Sarah and I get married,' Robert said nervously.

John stopped stamping and looked at his worker in some surprise. 'Married? You and Sarah?'

'Aye. We were hoping to go to church at the end of January. Sarah's mither has a room that we can use, now that her eldest lad has gone to Glasgae.'

'Oh. Right. Well, of course. Congratulations, young man. But why are you asking my permission?'

'Well, I thought that I should ask ye, as ye will likely lose Sarah as your dairy maid,' Robert explained.

'Oh. So Sarah will be leaving once you're married, then?'

'Aye.' Robert waited for another response from John.

John looked at the ground, then back at Robert. 'She's not with child, is she?'

'No, no, Mr Baird. We haven't ... well, ye ken, we havnae done anything carnal,' Robert protested.

'Oh. Good. Forgive me for asking, Robert,' John replied sheepishly. 'I understand that Sarah will want to leave once you start a family, but she could stay on as the dairy maid in the meantime, if that is what she wishes.'

'Aye, that's what we were hoping. Sarah always speaks very highly of Mrs Baird and yerself. She widnae want to leave you with a problem in the dairy.'

'You get yer wedding sorted, Robert, and you have oor best wishes,' John reassured Robert as he set off back to the house, thinking about the consequences of the news that he had just been told.

*

The weather in 1879 turned out to be one of the worst years on record. The snow continued to fall through April and into May. Snow even fell on the Cairngorms in June. The whole of northern Europe suffered from the cold and damp weather that lasted most of the year. Those crops that could be planted failed to ripen through lack of warmth and sunlight. Those farmers who managed to raise some cattle found that the prices that they were getting at market had fallen, owing to canned and refrigerated meat being shipped across from America. The coal companies chose this time to reduce the wages paid to their miners. There was a lot of unrest amongst the miners and a local coal miners' union was created to try to fight the wage cuts. Starvation took hold in many areas across the country.

CHAPTER FIFTEEN

July 1881

Margo Robertson had given birth to a son during the cold weather of 1879. Richard was, of course, thrilled to have his son, and he doted on the child. They named him David, after Richard's mentor in Dumfries, Richard having decided that he would not use his father's name, which would have been the custom. He had too many bad memories associated with his father's name and did not want his first son to be linked with them.

It was Margo who was first to notice David's unusual behaviour. Although he fed from the breast, it took him a long time to get him latched on for a feed. She also noticed that his eyes would often remain unfocused and would wander, rather than look at her face. As he grew older these unusual characteristics became more and more apparent, until eventually it was clear to Margo and Richard that their son had some type of problem functioning normally. They were, of course, devastated.

David was just over two years now. Although he had made some progress, he was a long way behind where one would expect to see a two-year-old child. His eye contact had improved and it was a great thrill to Margo when he managed a smile, but he could not stand and could barely crawl.

Flora and John's fourth son, Hugh, was now six months old and Flora had brought him over to visit Margo at her home in the apartment above the surgery.

'He's a bonnie laddie, Flora. You and wee Mary are getting outnumbered by boys up at the farm.'

'Aye. John's going to have plenty of help around the place in a few years' time. But it would have been nice to have another lassie.' Flora paused and glanced across at David, who was lying on his back, waving his arms around, on a rug in the corner of the room. She looked up at Margo. 'But, laddie or lassie, we want them healthy.'

'Aye. We do at that,' Margo replied quietly.

'How's he getting on? Have you noticed any improvements?'

'Och, Richard and I keep thinking that we see signs of improvements. He seems to be controlling his eye movements much better now. When I call his name he moves his eyes around looking for me, and he does smile when he sees me. I've tried to get him to sit up and I can feel that he is trying to use his muscles to stay upright, but he is still not strong enough to stay sitting. We were pleased when he managed to push himself up with his arms.'

'Has Richard had any success finding out what can be done for David?'

'He's been up to Edinburgh to consult the medical libraries at his old university and has spoken to some of his professors. Although there are some new therapies for adults with these abnormalities, there isn't really anything that has been tried on babies. Richard says that we will just have to see how he develops over the next few years,' Margo explained. 'We are lucky that we are able to look after him properly and have a maid who can help me with him. It gives me time with the girls. Richard was telling me that he has seen a couple of abnormal babies born in the rows, who seemed very healthy, but the next time he went to visit he was told that they had died. He suspected that the babies had been suffocated. Poor families cannot afford to waste time or food on a child who will not be productive. It's a cruel world, Flora.'

'Aye. Grace Houston was telling me a story that happened up at Garclaugh afore John and I took over. An Irish woman turned up at the door of James and Helen Houston, who were the tenants at that time. She was not only heavily pregnant, but she was in labour. Anyway, Helen and her maid got her sorted and helped deliver the bairn. The next morning they gave her a good meal and an auld shawl to wrap up the bairn, as it was cold weather. Then the woman left with the bairn. Well, the next day some boys fished the dead bairn out of the Nith, still wrapped in the shawl that Helen had given the woman. There was no sign of the mither and there never was.'

The two women sat in silence for a while, before Flora spoke. 'How's yer family dealing with it all?'

'Well, Mither keeps asking what could have caused the abnormalities.

She keeps trying to find a reason to explain why David is as he is. Could it be the polluted water? Perhaps it was the worry when the Glasgae bank collapsed? At least she hasn't suggested that it is a curse from God, like I have heard one of the auld nags say. The last time I took him oot for a walk I saw some women who I ken from the kirk cross to the other side of the street, rather than have to meet me and see the monster in the pram.' Margo tried to choke back a sob, but she could not hold it back any longer and she put her head in her hands and cried uncontrollably, her shoulders shaking. Flora knelt in front of her and hugged her tightly, as one would a hurt child.

Eventually Margo leaned back and took her handkerchief to dab her eyes. 'I'm sorry, Flora. I dinnae ken where that came from. I thought that I had shed all the tears that I had many months ago.'

'Wheesht. You get them out, Margo. I'm glad that you feel that you can share them with me.'

'You're a guid friend, Flora. In fact I feel that you are more like a sister at times.'

The two women hugged again.

*

Richard Robertson came out of the Castle Hotel, where he had been tending to a sick visitor. He almost walked straight into John, who was walking towards the church.

'Good morning, John,' Richard greeted him. 'It's not often we see you in toon during the week. What's got you all dressed up?'

'There's a meeting of the kirk elders that I have to attend, and Flora wanted to visit Margo with the new bairn.'

'How's wee Hugh getting on? No problems, I hope?' Richard enquired.

'No, he's fine. Strong as an ox.' John paused, wanting to ask about Richard's son, but feeling a twinge of guilt that he had four healthy sons and Richard's only son was not right. In the end he felt that Richard was anticipating the query, so he felt that he had to ask. 'How are you managing with yer lad, Richard?'

'Oh, he's a healthy wee laddie. He is making some progress, but it is very, very slow. Poor Margo feels so desperate that in some way it is her fault. It's not helped when some folk say it is a judgement from God for the distress caused by her faither's bank going bust.'

'Wheesht! Some folk have a cruel streak.' John looked beyond Richard to see another man walking towards them. It was Gilbert Sloan, who had lost all his money and his trading business when the Glasgow Bank went bankrupt. 'Talking about folk with a cruel streak, Gilbert Sloan is approaching.'

Richard muttered something under his breath that John could not hear, but John understood that he was not best pleased by the arrival.

'Good morning, gentlemen. I hope that the day is treating you both well,' Gilbert Sloan greeted John and Richard. They both replied with perfunctory greetings.

'It's a braw day, even if that cold wind is still around,' Gilbert went on. 'After last year's dreadful weather I thought that we would be due a good summer. I was looking across at Garclaugh this morning, Mr Baird, and saw that you have finished the hay making.'

John nodded. 'Aye. Despite the cold weather it has managed to stay dry, so we have got it all in without any bother. There was talk of it snowing up the hills further north. I heard that you have got back into trading again. How's yer new business going?'

'Aye, well, after the Glasgae Bank ruined me, I had to borrow money from my family to get started again.' Gilbert paused and looked at Richard. Richard stared resolutely ahead.

Margo's father had received a lot of abuse from Gilbert Sloan. Richard and Gilbert had had a very heated exchange of words, which Margo had worried would lead to a fight. Since then, the two men had avoided each other.

Concluding that he was not going to elicit a reaction this time from Richard, Gilbert continued. 'It's doing quite well. It will tak me a while yet to get back to where I was afore I lost everything. I am working with my cousin in Ayr and we hope to get involved in shipping wheat from America. There's money to be made in that business.'

'Shipping wheat, eh?' John asked. 'With Disraeli gone we could do with some politicians in London who are willing to reintroduce the Corn Laws. But Disraeli spent too much time fighting battles with Afghanistan and Russia, and not enough time fighting for oor farmers.'

Gilbert Sloan tensed and Richard could see his face flushing with anger. 'Reintroducing the Corn Laws is not going to help the poor folk in Scotland. Why should they have to spend what little money that they have to buy expensive bread, because Scottish farmers cannot produce it as cheaply as in America?'

'It wasn't the American farmers who kept the poor folk from starving last year; it was the Scottish farmers struggling in wet and cold fields,' John retorted.

'I don't think that this is the time or the place to argue the merits of the Corn Laws,' Richard intervened. 'I've got some patients to see, so I will have to bid farewell.'

'Aye. I have to collect Flora and get back to Garclaugh,' John added, relieved to have an excuse to get away from Gilbert Sloan.

John and Richard walked on towards the church, where Reverend Murray was standing watching them approach. He was with another man, who John was trying to recognise, as his face seemed familiar.

Reverend Murray greeted them as they approached. 'Mr Baird, Dr Robertson. I hope that you and your families are both well?'

John and Richard thanked Reverend Murray and shook his hand.

'I don't know if you have met Mr James Stevenson,' Reverend Murray said. 'He moved into Nether Cairn Farm on the Kirkconnel road last year and has joined the congregation here. James, this is John Baird and Dr Richard Robertson, who both moved into New Cumnock about ten years ago. Would that be correct, gentlemen?'

'It was 1869 that I came here, so it will be twelve years,' Richard said. 'I believe it was a couple of years before that you moved into Garclaugh, John?'

'Aye, 1866,' replied John. 'I haven't been formally introduced, but I have seen you in kirk and have heard yer name mentioned. I believe that you are a relative of the Stevensons at Tarbolton?'

'Aye. I was born at Lady Yard Farm. My faither was Allan. There are plenty of Stevensons over that way. Almost as many as the Bairds up at Sorn.' James chuckled.

'Would you be any relative of the surveyor Allan Stevenson who built the bridge on Mansfield Road?' John asked.

'Aye, he's my eldest brother's son. A bright lad who managed to get out of farming and has set himself up as an architect in Ayr, as well as a road surveyor.'

'So, how are things going over on the hillside on the Cairn?' John asked James.

Richard interrupted before James could reply. 'Well, afore you two farmers start comparing the size of yer coos' udders, I'm afeared that I am going to have to leave you. I have to get back to the surgery.'

As Richard began to leave, the Reverend Murray took a couple of quick steps over to him and caught his elbow, leaving the two farmers in conversation.

'Richard. I was hoping that you might have time for a word or twa.' Reverend Murray looked hopefully at Richard.

'Of course, Reverend. Will ye walk with me back to the surgery? You have tickled my interest.'

'It's about the miners, Richard. I was over at Connel Park this morning and there is a lot of anger over the wage cuts. I met with James Armstrong at the Bank Free Kirk and he was saying the same. I ken that ye still visit the rows to help oot, and I wondered if it is just Connel Park or all the rows where there is unrest.'

'There is always anger at the rows, Reverend, and quite rightly so. Ye ken my feelings aboot the conditions that the miners have to endure. I have spoken aboot them often enough. But you're right; there is a lot more anger just now. There's a young chap who was appointed secretary of the Ayrshire Miners' Association last year. Kier Hardie is his name. He's been speaking to the miners and pushing for them to strike. I widnae be at all surprised if they were to come oot on strike soon. For all the good that it would do.'

'Oh. I see. Do you ken if this chap Hardie has spoken to the owners?'

'I'm sure that he has been trying to speak to all the owners or their managers,' Richard said. 'But the owners are the ones who got together to lower their wages in the first place. I can't see them pushing them back up again at the threat of a strike. They will enter discussions and drag them on in the winter, so that it is too cold for the miners to strike.'

'What do you mean, "too cold for the miners to strike"?'

'If ye go oot on strike in the summer and have no wages, then ye can go into the fields and catch some conies or pick berries and cobnuts. In winter there is no food in the fields, except if ye steal neeps. So if ye are going to strike, it's best to do it in the summer,' Richard explained.

'I see. You sound as if you want them to strike.'

'I want them to have a decent wage and be given decent homes that are not so damp that it is a miracle if the wains reach five years old, Reverend,' Richard stated.

'I know, Richard. We all want that for the miners, but a strike will bring real misery and hardship to all the community. There will be thieving and violence.'

They had reached the front of the surgery. Richard paused and stood in the road.

'What do you want me to do, Reverend?' he asked.

'If I arrange a meeting with William Hyslop, would ye join me to speak with him?'

Richard threw out a sarcastic laugh. 'William Hyslop! He's not much better than his faither. We had hoped that when he inherited the company two years ago he might improve things, but what happened? He reduced the miners' wages. No, Reverend, you don't want me at such a meeting, as I might not be able to control my tongue.'

Before Reverend Murray could persist with his request, Margo appeared from the door of the house with wee Hugh, followed by Flora. Margo spoke across to Reverend Murray, as she passed Hugh back to his mother. 'It sounds, Reverend, as if you have just spoken to Richard about the lot of the miners. You are a brave man to raise that topic.'

'You are quite right, Mrs Robertson. But Richard is blessed with true Christian concern for his fellow man. I wish that more of our community shared his concerns; then we might make the whole toon a more Christian place. I'll need to get back to the meeting at the kirk; they will be wondering where I have gone. Good day to you, ladies. Richard.' Reverend Murray turned and walked briskly back in the direction of the church, his black coattails flapping behind him.

Richard watched him before turning to Flora. 'I left John talking to another farmer who has moved into the area recently. Mr James Stevenson was his name. How are ye getting back to Garclaugh, Flora?'

'John said he would leave the break at the Castle Hotel, so I will walk back up there. John will walk back and call in at Castlemains Farm on the way. He wants to have a look at one of their bulls. Ye ken John; if he's no thinking about coos, he's thinking about bulls,' Flora replied, to a burst of shared laughter between the three friends.

*

As Richard had predicted, the coal companies dragged discussions on until the autumn, when the miners finally were persuaded, by a very vocal and passionate Kier Hardie, to go out on strike. The strike lasted ten weeks before the miners went back to work, without their demands for a 10% wage rise being met. Kier Hardie was sacked as secretary of the Ayrshire Miners' Association, but not long afterwards the coal companies decided to prevent future strike action by giving the miners a modest pay rise. Kier Hardie went on to take up journalism and wrote for the *Cumnock News*, a paper loyal to the pro-worker Liberal Party.

Despite John's hopes for warmer weather, the cold weather continued through to the autumn. Harvest could not start until the first week of October and much of the corn was cut green. As a result of the poor harvest, Gilbert Sloan's venture into buying grain from America would bring him good profits, whilst the local farmers would have another winter when they struggled to find fodder for their animals. It's an ill wind that blows nobody good.

CHAPTER SIXTEEN

July 1883

Wee John was no longer one of the new children at the school, as he was now six years old and had been at school for a year. This meant that he could go and play in the yard with the older children, rather than be minded by one of the school helpers. He was playing a chasing game with his friends, Walter Steel and Will Howatt, when, whilst turning around to look at his chasers, he ran straight into one of the bigger boys. This bigger boy was George Sloan, who his brother Tom had warned him to avoid. Wee John had heard tales of the fights that had taken place between Tom and George, which usually ended in both boys receiving hefty bruises and neither accepting the other boy as the winner.

As George picked himself up off the ground where John had knocked him, George's friends gathered around the pair. They wore smiles in anticipation of watching some bullying action.

'I'm sorry, George,' John said nervously.

'You're Tom Baird's little brother, aren't you?' George enquired menacingly.

John nodded.

George took a step forward and grabbed John's arm. 'And Tom is not around to help you.'

Tom had left school when he had reached the age of twelve. Fortunately for Tom and unfortunately for John, George Sloan was slightly younger, so he was still at the school tormenting other children.

'Leave me alone!' John said loudly, struggling to free himself. Walt and Will were standing close by, not quite knowing whether to step in to help or run away. 'I dinnae mean to dunt ye,' John wailed.

'It's nearly time to go back to class, Baird. Have ye bin to the cludgie yet?' George started to pull John towards the toilet block that was positioned towards the back of the school playground.

New Cumnock School 1909.
From a postcard (www.newcumnock.net)

George pushed John into the toilet block and then grabbed the back of his head, pushing John's face towards the hole in the wooden board that was fixed above the long drop toilet. John planted his hands on either side of the hole in the wooden board and straightened his arms to stop his head being pushed into the hole.

'What's going on in here, then?' a man's voice boomed outside the toilet.

George immediately let go of John and stepped away, changing his face from a snarl to an innocent smile. 'Nothing. I was just showing John Baird where the cludgie is,' he said to the figure of Mr Stirling, the second master, who had appeared in the toilet doorway.

'You're a liar as well as a bully, George Sloan. Now get to yer class afore I put the tawse on ye.'

The tawse was a leather strap that was used throughout Scottish schools to administer corporal punishment. It was produced by saddle-makers especially for its purpose and consisted of two parallel strips of leather attached to a handle. The tawse was usually administered to the hands of girls and the bottoms of boys and was feared by all the children.

The crowd of boys quickly dispersed and John joined Walt and Will. George looked menacingly across at John as Mr Stirling escorted him across the playground back to the main school.

'You were saved then, John,' said Walt.

'Yer sister Mary went and found Mr Stirling,' Will added.

'Aye, well, he was lucky that Mr Stirling arrived as I was about to stamp on his foot.' John tried to put a brave face on, but tears were not far from his eyes. He would have to keep his eyes open when he was in the playground again and keep well clear of George Sloan.

*

Flora was towards the end of her sixth pregnancy and was being examined by Richard Robertson at the surgery. He was leaning over Flora's abdomen, using a short brass Pinard horn to his ear to listen for the baby's heartbeat. After a while he straightened and used his fingers to probe around the enlarged bump. Eventually he stepped away and returned the horn to his desk.

'The bairn's heartbeat is much lower than we would expect, which would suggest it may well be in a breech position,' he said. 'I think it would be a good idea if you were to come into the surgery when your pains start and we will deliver the bairn here.'

'If that's what ye think, then that is what I will do, Richard,' Flora replied. 'I'll make sure that John has the horse and the trap ready to bring me over.'

'I'll get Margo to make oor guest bedroom ready; it will be more comfortable than using the operating room, and I am sure that Margo will want to make a fuss of ye as well.'

Flora got up in an ungainly manner from the examination table and began to button up her dress. She then collected her coat, and Richard accompanied her out of the house and onto the pavement. They both looked down the road towards Bridgend, where there was the noise of hammering and workmen.

'They are macadamising the road.' Richard explained, anticipating Flora's query. 'Since this section of road is often damp and stays muddy, the council have decided to grade it from the bridge up to Castle. I'm glad that the council are taking their new responsibilities seriously now the tolls have finished and they have control over the roads.'

'It's a fine noise that they are making,' Flora said. 'I wouldn't want to be next to that all day.'

'Aye, and it's going to be a real nuisance when they get down here to the hoose,' Richard said. He pulled his fob watch from his waistcoat pocket and noted the time. 'You'll be collecting the wains from school, then?'

'Aye. They'll be oot soon. I'll walk over and meet them, then we'll go over to Hugh Baird, the farrier. Rob is getting some new shoes put on the horse.'

'That'll be Robert Burnett, your horseman?' Richard asked. 'I met Sarah in toon yesterday. They have twa fine boys now. She was telling me that they have got a cottage.'

'Aye. John loaned them some money for a deposit. Rob's a good worker and John wants him to stay on at the farm. He has a real way with the horses. Do ye ken that he talks to them? All the time ye hear him blethering on to them. I'll swear that they talk back to him!' she said, laughing.

Richard chuckled. 'It's how to keep them calm. I'll talk to my horse quite often as well. Ye should try it, Flora.'

Flora walked along the road and up to the gates of the school. A couple of other mothers were waiting to take their children back home, but most of the children found their own way home. Some had a long walk up into the hills, a walk that could take them well over an hour. She did not know any of the mothers very well, so she smiled and greeted them but did not start a conversation. She stood waiting, listening to their chatter.

'Have ye heard that they're building a new Catholic school?' one mother said.

'Aye. Well, it's all these Irish working in the mines. My Jack was saying that they are building more rows at Connel Park. It's getting like a new toon over there now,' another replied.

'They could do with building some more bothies, so that the miners keep oot of the toon at the weekend. Every Saturday night there seems to be a drunken fight in toon between groups of miners.'

Flora was glad that she lived on the farm, well away from the Saturday night brawls. Margo had mentioned the rowdiness that occurred on some nights as drunken miners staggered back to their homes.

Wee John was first to appear from the school door and he walked over towards the school gate, but he did not see Flora. A larger boy appeared a moment later and, as he walked past John, Flora saw him snarl words at John, who shrank away. Flora went towards the gate, and as the boy walked past she gave him a stare. George Sloan looked back, sneered and then walked on.

'Who's that unpleasant young man?' Flora asked John. John did not reply.

'That's George Sloan,' the voice of John's sister, Mary, chirped behind him. 'He was bullying John at lunchtime, but Mr Stirling came and stopped it.'

'Is that right?' Flora watched the retreating figure of George Sloan, who had now been joined by a couple of his friends. She looked down at John and she could see the frightened little boy inside the brave exterior. 'Never ye mind, John. Let's collect Andrew and we will walk o'er to the farrier. Hopefully ye can watch the blacksmith making some horseshoes. We can also watch the workmen making the new road.'

A big smile broke across John's face.

The family group walked and skipped down past the front of the school, towards the men working on the road. There were a couple of carts, one loaded with small stones, the other empty and waiting to be refilled from a local quarry. There were a team of men gathering around the stones that had been tipped from the cart. They were hammering at large stones to break them into smaller pieces, as the macadam road-building method required fairly small stones. The workmen had been told that the stones had to be small enough to fit into their mouths.

Most of the workmen were older men or had handicaps of some sort. There was one man who only had one arm, but he swung his hammer as well as the other men. It was hard, low-paid work, but it was the only work that some of these men could get, as the coal mines and farms only wanted the fully fit men. There were plenty of young and fit men coming over from Ireland and down from the Highlands, so work on the roads was welcomed by those men who would otherwise be struggling to find regular jobs.

As Flora and the children walked towards Hugh Baird's smithy, the hammering of the stones was replaced by the hammering of metal. Rob Burnett was outside the building in a small yard where he was starting to get the horse back into the shafts of the break. Andrew ran on ahead to help him.

The shed doors were wide open, exposing the innards of the smithy. In the centre, at the heart of the building, was a forge on which a heap of coke glowed orange. Air was being blown in bursts from a fan, which caused the central orange glow to become an intense yellow, beneath a crust of cooler and darker pieces of coke. Sparks were thrown out by the blasts of air, sounding and looking as if a dragon were breathing somewhere in the darkness behind the forge. John and Mary were transfixed by the collection of small blue flames that danced above the hot coals and then disappeared into wisps of smoke that rose slowly, then increasingly quickly, into the chimney.

A young man was working to the side of the forge, hammering on a long rod of metal. He turned and smiled when he saw Flora and the children. This was James Sheel, Hugh Baird's grandson, whom Hugh had trained to take over his business one day.

James plunged the rod of metal into the hot fire, sending more sparks and smoke into the space around the forge. The roof above the forge rose up in a cone, allowing the smoke to exit through a brick chimney. On each side of the forge were work benches on which a large array of tools lay ready for the strong hands of James and his grandfather to grab when needed. Other tools hung from hooks on the walls behind the benches: hammers, tongs and various chains.

James saw wee John staring at the forge. 'Do ye want to help me make a horseshoe?' he asked.

John looked at his mother with pleading eyes.

Flora looked over to James. 'He's a bit wee to be working so close to the forge, isn't he?'

'He can help me hammer the rod. He'll be fine, Mrs Baird. I'll look after him.'

Reluctantly, Flora gave John a little push in his back towards James.

James had taken the rod of metal, which by now was glowing orange, and placed it on the anvil. 'Get a hammer from the bench,' he told John.

John went across to the bench and put both hands around the handle of the largest hammer he could see. He tried to lift it but could only drag it closer to the edge.

James laughed. 'Just get the smaller yen.'

John lifted a smaller hammer and turned towards the anvil.

'Now then,' James said, 'just hit the metal rod right on the top.'

John lifted the hammer and tentatively tapped the metal rod on the top.

'Harder than that, John!'

John used both hands to lift the hammer and struck the rod several times, making it bend over the cone at the end of the anvil.

'That'll do. Well done. Now, you stand back with yer mither and I'll show you how we do the job properly.' James set about hammering the metal rod into a curve that would eventually become a horseshoe, like the ones that had been fitted to the horse that Rob and Andrew were busy getting harnessed onto the break.

Once the harnessing was completed, Rob helped Flora climb into the break to join the children, who were already squeezed onto the wooden bench. They travelled towards Castle, heading back to Garclaugh.

As they reached the top of Castle, Rob turned to Flora. 'Have you heard that the steeple on the auld kirk has collapsed?'

'Och! I hope that no one was hurt,' Flora replied.

'Not that I've heard tell.'

'Well, the kirk has been neglected for the past fifty years,' Flora said. 'It's in a poor fettle and it's only going to get worse. The stanes in the kirkyard are in a dreadful state and there is no room for more burials. Reverend Murray is going to have to find somewhere else to bury folk.'

'Aye. I have heard folk say that there is a right reek that comes from new graves during the hot weather,' said Rob. 'They say that the good Lord will provide, but He seems to be taking His time aboot it.'

'Wheesht, Rob. Don't ye tak the Lord's name in vain,' Flora chided. 'It's not for us to question His plans for us.'

'I'm sorry, Mrs Baird. I didnae mean to speak agin the Lord,' Rob replied sheepishly.

The rest of the journey continued in silence, except for Andrew and

Mary whispering to each other. Flora heard Andrew tell his sister to keep something a secret.

'Aye, and what are you twa scheming?' she asked them.

'Andrew and his friends are going to look for gold up on Craigs,' Mary announced, to Andrew's obvious annoyance.

'Looking for gold?' Flora asked in surprise.

'Aye, they want to see if there are any more gold coins like the shepherd found last year,' Mary replied.

Rob and Flora looked at each other and laughed.

'Well, do ye ken where he found them, Andrew?' Flora asked.

Andrew shook his head.

'Well, it's a big hill to look for gold. There's been plenty of folk searching, including the shepherd who found the hoard.'

Andrew looked deflated. 'Is it true that he got eighty English pounds and got to keep some of the coins, Maw?'

'That's what they say, Andrew. He's a rich man now.'

'But there might be some more gold coins up there,' Andrew said.

'No, Andrew. Ye're not going up Craigs with your friends. If ye have so much energy to want to walk up Glen Afton to the Blackcraig Hill, then I am sure that yer faither can find ye plenty of work to do on the farm.' Flora ended the discussion.

Andrew kept quiet as he knew that his mother was correct when she said his father would find them work to do. His father always had a long list of jobs that he wanted his children to do, even the young ones.

CHAPTER SEVENTEEN

August 1883

The explosion of a volcano called Krakatoa on the other side of the world barely made the front page of the *Ayr Advertiser*, but the glorious red sunsets and sunrises that appeared over Scotland some months later certainly caught people's attention. The gas and dust thrown into the Earth's atmosphere by the explosion spread around the world and eventually caused average temperatures to drop by two degrees. Having already had nearly a decade of cold and wet weather, a drop in temperature was yet another burden that the farmers in Nithsdale would have to tolerate.

John was getting dressed more slowly than usual, partly because he was gazing at the red sunrise and partly because Flora had been more restless than normal during the early hours and was fairly certain that the baby was on its way.

'Do ye want me to get the break ready or not?' he asked.

'Aye. I'm fairly sure that things are happening. Just give me a help in case my waters go. I don't want to mess the bed.'

John helped Flora get out of bed, then waited as she breathed sharply at a strong contraction.

'Aye, that's definite. I'll get the break sorted,' said John as he pulled up his breeks and pulled the braces over his shoulders. 'I'll get Jane to sort out the wains and Tom to get the coos in.' Jane Calder was the new housemaid.

Rob Burnett had not yet arrived, so John got the horse from its stable and took it over to where the break was ready to be harnessed up. Rob usually did this work, and it took John a little while to get all the leather straps positioned properly and the shafts of the break lifted up into place. Flora was standing by the house door with her bag when he finally finished and led the horse over to the house.

John helped Flora get into the break and then he gave various instructions to Tom about what needed to be done around the farm. Tom was now thirteen years old and a capable lad around the farm. He was excited about this opportunity to take his father's place as the boss.

It was getting much lighter when they arrived at the surgery, and the town was waking up. Various shopkeepers were opening up, and the smell of fresh bread, as they passed the bakery, made John realise that they had left home without eating. His stomach rumbled at the thought of breakfast.

Richard's maid helped Flora down from the break. Flora had to pause on the way to the front door as another contraction arrived.

Margo met her in the hallway. 'Come now, Flora, let's get ye comfortable upstairs in oor spare room.' She helped Flora up the stairs and settled her onto the bed.

Meanwhile the maid showed John into the surgery waiting room. After about ten minutes some loud footsteps coming down the stairs announced the arrival of Richard.

'Good morning, John, and what a spectacular sunrise to greet ye this morning,' Richard greeted John. He continued without giving John time to respond. 'Flora is now comfortable upstairs and her contractions are coming fairly regularly, so I would expect the bairn to be arriving this morning. Now, ye'll be aware that we are fairly certain that the bairn is breech. This means that instead of coming oot head first, it will be coming oot feet first. This can cause some difficulties, but we are well prepared and I am sure that we'll be able to sort out any problems.'

'Aye. Well, I'll call in at the kirk and say some prayers that all will be well,' John responded.

'You'll have something to eat first, though. Come upstairs to oor rooms and join us for breakfast.'

John joined Richard and his family around the breakfast table. Since the birth of David with his problems, Margo had had another boy called Richard who, thankfully, was perfectly normal. John sat amongst the chattering children as the maid rushed around trying to make sure that there was enough food for everyone. At one stage Margo appeared, put her hand on John's shoulder and told him that Flora was fine and had had something to eat.

The day was one that John and Flora would always remember. As Richard had predicted, the birth was not at all easy and the baby was breech. During the latter part of the delivery, the baby's head became stuck and Richard desperately tried to free it as he watched the baby turning blue. Eventually the baby arrived, but Richard was afraid that their efforts had been in vain, as the baby took a long time to take his first breath and to change to a healthy pink. After a while, the infant cried and he seemed to recover well. Richard was thankful that he had persuaded Flora to come to the surgery for the delivery.

John had returned to the farm for a few hours during the morning, but had spent the rest of the day fretfully pacing around in the Robertsons' living room. He was mightily relieved to join an exhausted-looking Flora and their new son, William.

*

The autumn drew closer and the harvest began. Rob had hitched up two of the Clydesdale horses to a reaper machine to cut the oats. The reaper was a wheeled machine that was pulled by the horses, whilst the driver sat on a metal sprung seat at the back, next to one wheel. To the right of the driver was a platform with the second wheel on its edge. To the front of the platform lay a set of reciprocating blades that were driven by gears connected to the wheel. So, as the machine was pulled forward, the blades would cut the corn close to the ground and the cut corn stalks would then fall back onto the platform. As the stalks accumulated on the platform, a rotating rake, also driven from the wheel gearing, would sweep down to push a bundle of cut stalks from the back of the platform onto the ground behind the reaper. Men and women walking behind the machine would then only have to pick up the cut corn in their arms, use a twist of stalks to tie the bundle and prop it upright into a stook. These stooks would stand in rows along the field and then, once dry, would be collected onto a wagon and taken into one of the barns or made into large ricks. Come the wintertime the corn stooks would be taken from the ricks and be threshed to knock out the grain.

Harvest time always involved plenty of labour, and farmers would hire in workers to help stook the corn and make it into ricks. Often whole families would be out in the fields as this task was more important than schooling or other chores. School holidays were set because these were the times when the children were required to help on the farms.

It was no different at Meikle Garclaugh. Tom, at fourteen, was old enough to be out on the farm doing as many jobs as the employed men, and even Andrew, at eleven, was expected to take on some of the lighter jobs. Both had grown up surrounded by horses and could handle the Clydesdale horses with confidence. The Clydesdales were more compact draught horses than Shire horses, which made them more suitable for the small fields found in Scotland. They were also quiet and calm animals, so they were easy to handle. All of the adult horses at Garclaugh had the white faces and white feathered lower legs which were now recognised as breed characteristics by the newly established Clydesdale Horse Society.

Whilst Tom preferred to be out in the fields with the horses, Andrew enjoyed working with the cows and helping Catherine Bruce, the new dairy maid, with the milking. Although he did not yet have the strength in his hands to be able to milk as fast as Catherine, he helped to carry the pails of milk to the dairy and pour them into the steel milk churns.

Two Clydesdale Horses.
Original photograph courtesy of Terry Harrison

Andrew had a calm manner around the cows and had already learned all their names. He also knew most of the dams and sires of the cows, certainly the younger ones.

Flora would often smile to hear Andrew discussing the cows and their breeding with John. In order for a milk cow to continue to produce milk she needs to become pregnant and have a calf, so each year the cow must be mated with a bull, usually eight weeks after she has given birth. John selected the bull for siring according to its breeding characteristics. These could only be determined by studying the offspring that were produced. If the calves sired by a particular bull grew and became good milk cows, then the bull would be used more often. A bull calf born to a good cow and sired by a good bull would be a valuable animal that could be sold or rented out to other farmers for breeding.

John had high hopes for the dairy cows and bulls that he was breeding. He had formed a good relationship with another farmer in Mauchline, Robert Wallace, who was also breeding prize Ayrshire cattle. They often met to discuss possible matings and John was keen to use one or two of Robert's bulls, for which he would have to pay a high price.

*

As baby William got older Flora began to notice some worrying signs that all was not functioning right. He did not grip with his hands like Flora had expected, and his limb movements were very stiff and uncontrolled. She feared that he may have suffered during the protracted birth and that he could have a similar problem to Richard and Margo's boy David. She kept these troubling thoughts to herself for many weeks, until one day Margo came to visit her at the farm.

It was a cold day in February and William was lying on a rug in front of the fire in the living room. Margo had brought her daughters Ellen and Annie with her, as well as her own new baby Richard, who was now eighteen months old and very lively.

'Wee Richard is certainly keeping ye active,' Flora noted, as Margo had had to get up to stop him crawling off down the corridor to the kitchen for a third time.

'Aye. He's so different to the girls when they were wee; they tended to stay put when ye put them doon. I suppose that is just boys,' Margo replied.

'Aye, you may be right,' Flora replied in a distracted way. 'Margo. Ye know that I am nae one for small talk. I asked you to come over because I wanted to talk to you about William. I don't think that he is right. He seems to be so like your David.'

'Aye. I've noticed, Flora. I noticed a while back, but didnae want to say anything to ye in case I was wrong.'

'I havnae said anything to John, but I am sure that he's noticed as well. We all seem to be keeping our fears secret from each other, Margo. We need to discuss this properly. Can you ask Richard if he would come over on Sunday after kirk and have a look at him?' Flora asked.

'Aye. I'll ask him, Flora. But you ken that there may not be anything that he can do to make William better?'

'Aye, Margo. We've spent enough time with you and Richard as you have searched for a treatment for David. I ken what the situation might be.'

*

Time for Flora seemed to drag on slowly as she waited for Sunday and the visit of Richard. She had at last managed to talk with John about her worries and found that, as she suspected, he had noticed that all did not seem right with William.

Richard examined William carefully before he confirmed to John and Flora that William seemed to lack coordination of his limbs and his muscles were weak. He suspected that William's brain had been starved of oxygen during the protracted and difficult delivery.

Richard spoke quietly. 'I'm so sorry, Flora.'

'Wheesht, Richard! It's not your fault. It's God's will,' said John. 'If you had not noticed that the baby was breech before he was born, then it could have been much worse. The birth could have taken Flora as well.'

'Aye. It's true, Richard. Do not blame yerself. We have to get on and see how the wee laddie grows. He may turn out to surprise everyone,' Flora proclaimed bravely, whilst struggling to hold back a flood of tears. 'It seems that our two families have been brought together to share the problems of raising our damaged children,' she managed to say, before the tears came to her eyes. She looked at William, who was happily waving his arms on the rug and smiling. 'Poor wee mite.'

CHAPTER EIGHTEEN

July 1888

At Meikle Garclaugh Flora was as busy as ever around the house: a house that was now increasingly filled with the noise of children. She had given birth to another boy called Gilbert, who was healthy, normal and now three years old. William was now five years old and required constant supervision. He could now sit up and could move around on his bottom, but could not stand up for any length of time. He could recognise his family and smiled when his siblings spoke to him. They were still struggling to teach him to feed himself and control his bladder, which created a lot of work for Flora and for Jean Anderson, the nursemaid who had been taken on to help look after him.

Tom was now eighteen years old and was a regular farmhand learning to look after the cattle and the horses, as well as to tackle the many other jobs that farms generated. Rob Burnett had left a couple of years before with his wife Sarah, in order to take a new job on a farm near Kilmarnock. John was pleased that Rob had taught Tom many of the basic skills required by a good ploughman and Tom was looking forward to competing in his first ploughing match. Andrew, at fourteen years old, had continued his interest in the cows and could regularly be found with them in the byre.

As the Garclaugh herd had gained in reputation, John was taking some of his cows and bulls to shows around the West of Scotland. The local cattle fair that used to take place on Castle Green had ceased, but there were more prestigious shows organised by the Highland and Agricultural Society of Scotland. Andrew helped his father prepare the cows and young bulls by washing and brushing their coats. He would then lead them to the station, where they would be put onto trains that would take them to Ayr, Dumfries or Kilmarnock: wherever the agricultural shows were being held. The prize that a cow or bull might be awarded at one of these shows would then be used to advertise and sell its offspring at a higher price.

Although Flora was not keen for Mary to work as a dairy maid, the demands of milking cows and producing cheeses meant that Mary would be expected to help out at busy times. Catherine Bruce had left and a new dairy maid called Maggie Annand had been taken on. John had met her at the hiring fair at Cumnock in March and she had seemed to be very suitable. The hiring fairs were becoming less important as farmers now tended to offer longer contracts to workers, but some farm workers still liked the flexibility of moving from one farm to another, even though there was no guarantee of regular work. For some young women it gave an opportunity to find a suitable husband and marry into a farming family, and in Ayrshire there was always a demand for good dairy maids. Some farmers had been known to make their sons marry a good dairy maid in order to keep her skills on the farm.

*

Richard Robertson and John Baird were standing next to each other in the small crowd that was assembling in front of the town church and the newly built town hall. In the courtyard to the front of the hall a brass band was getting prepared. A small wooden platform had been erected to one side and there were some ribbons and flowers decorating a lectern, in anticipation of the arrival of the dignitaries who would officially open the town hall.

'I thought that you would be too busy this morning to watch the opening,' John said to Richard. 'I thought that you did not approve of all this pomp.'

'Well, I'm not such a rebellious youngster any more, John,' Richard replied, 'and I have been asked to sit on the management board for the hall, so I am obliged to be here for the opening. This will be a fine community facility and I approve.'

'It's a shame that it wasn't completed for the Queen's Golden Jubilee last year. If the council had added to all the private contributions then it could have been. Perhaps we could have then asked Her Majesty to open it and called it the Queen Victoria Jubilee Hall?' John chuckled at his own remark.

'You may laugh, John, but that suggestion was considered. Since she hardly ever leaves Osborne House, I don't think she would have made it all the way up to New Cumnock just to open oor wee toon hall.'

'You didnae ask your friend Kier Hardie to come and open it, then?' John asked.

'Nay. I don't think he would want to come to an event such as this. If it was a community hall for the miners then he might consider it.'

'So what mischief is he creating just now? I would have thought that the thrashing that he got in the Mid Lanarkshire by-election in April would have quietened him doon somewhat, but I was reading in the *Advertiser* that he is calling a big public meeting in Glasgae. What's that all aboot, then?'

'He and Robert Graham plan to set up a political party for the working people of Scotland,' Richard said. 'They want to call it the Scottish Labour Party. It's a bold plan and I support it. It's about time that there was someone speaking up for the working people, Gladstone certainly doesn't do anything, for all his party's fine words about supporting ordinary working folk.'

'Aye, well, so long as his miners and other working folk have not got the vote, he'll find it hard to get into Parliament.'

'If Hardie can do anything to make it safer for the miners then he will get my vote. You'll remember that there were eighty miners killed at the Udston pit at Hamilton last year, John.'

'There is no question that he's trying to improve things for the miners. I've heard that he's a godly man and that he's one of these folk that won't touch a dram.'

'Aye, he's always bin a member of the temperance movement. Did ye ken that he was working as a trapper doon a mine at ten years auld? He's experienced the life of a miner, unlike some of these other Liberal politicians who just talk aboot being working men. I widnae be at all surprised if this Scottish Labour Party gets a lot of support.'

'Well, we will just have to wait and see,' John replied quickly, in the hope that he could stop Richard going off on one of his long, passionate rants about the poor conditions of working miners.

As the two men waited, a crowd of councillors, their wives and other officials started to assemble. Soon the conductor signalled the band, who stood up and began to play a rousing tune to welcome the start of

New Cumnock Church and Town Hall

proceedings. The Marquis of Bute was asked to do the official opening and he gave a short speech, then the leader of the parish council gave a speech that was so long that someone in the crowd shouted for him to 'get on with it'. After he finished, the Reverend Murray stood up and said a prayer and blessed the new hall.

'It is good to see that Robert Murray is still officiating at some events. I thought that James Millar would have taken over completely by now,' Richard remarked.

'I think that he's finding it hard to let go. Young James will just have to be patient,' John replied.

'Have you heard that James has been campaigning to get a new graveyard found? He says that the auld one is full up and that the smell of putrefaction in the auld graveyard is too much. The heritors have been asked to pay for one.'

The Reverend James Millar had been brought to the church to help Reverend Murray, who at seventy years old was finding being the minister hard work. Robert Murray had felt that young James, at only twenty-eight, needed further 'hands-on' training, despite James having a theology degree. Two years on and James's training was still progressing, although most of the congregation were very happy with the way that he carried out his tasks and particularly enjoyed his lively sermons.

The heritors were the ancient landowners in Scotland. Often they were, and still are, absent landlords who were forced, through Scottish parliamentary acts in the seventeenth century, to take responsibility for providing churches, churchyards, ministers, schools and school masters for their parishes. Landowners such as the Hyslops, the Menteaths and the Marquis of Bute were heritors. When the new church was built, the heritors were allowed to have pews allocated especially for them, although during most services their pews remained empty. Lady Jane Menteath, being one of the few local heritors who regularly attended the church, used her family's pew.

The band played another tune and the dignitaries made their way into the town hall, where tea and cakes were being served. They were quickly followed by the other guests and onlookers who entered in the hope that they too would be able to partake of the tea and cakes. John and Richard stayed on their spot close to the church as the crowd around them dispersed.

'So what has brought you into toon, John?' Richard asked.

'As a kirk elder I thought that I should make an appearance, and I had some business at the bank. Also Flora asked if she could visit Margo,' John explained. 'Perhaps we should make oor way doon to yer hoose and meet up with oor wives?'

The two men left the scene of the opening, which by now was empty apart from a scattering of children and some band members who were still packing away their instruments, and they set off down the road to the surgery.

On the way down to the surgery they saw James Stevenson, whom John had met on a number of occasions at various cattle markets and shows.

'Good day, Dr Robertson and John. It seems that I have missed the opening of the toon hall,' James greeted the two friends.

'Aye. The speeches are all done, but if yer sharp, you might find yen or twa sandwiches still left on a plate,' John teased.

James laughed easily with them. 'John, I am interested in using one of yer bulls. I wondered if I could come over one day to have a look at some.'

'Aye. Ye wud be most welcome. Come over any time,' John replied. 'If I am not around my son Andrew wud be able to show ye the bulls and tell ye of their pedigrees. He may look like a scholar, but he's got a lot of knowledge packed in his head.'

The two men shook hands and James promised to visit in the next few days.

*

Flora had decided to miss the opening of the town hall in order to visit Margo in her apartment above the surgery.

'How's all your wains, Margo?'

'They're all well. Although Jane is not a wain any more; she's quite the young lady. She's up at my mither's hoose just now, as my sister is visiting with her wains. It's so easy for Lizzie to get the train down from Muirkirk. Wee Robert is the only one at home now; the others are all at school. It's strange to think that Richard and I were so keen to have a laddie and now we have had three in a row.'

'How's yer Annie?' Flora enquired. 'You were worried about her cough the last time I spoke to you.'

'Not so good, Flora. Richard is fairly certain that she is in the early stage of TB. We are giving her plenty of fresh food and trying to get her to rest. Richard wants to take her up the glen when the weather warms up to get some clean air into her lungs. It's a worry,' Margo replied.

'And how are you managing David?' Flora asked.

'With difficulty. He's a big seven-year-old lad and when you lift him it's like lifting a dead weight. We've hired another lassie to come and help us, but they don't stay long. They don't like to do all the changing of his dirty clothes.' Margo paused. 'Are you making any progress with William?'

'He still wets himself quite often, but at least he seems to be getting the idea of what he's supposed to do on the toilet,' Flora replied. 'We've made a frame for him to sit for a while on the pot and he usually manages to do something. He's a happy laddie, despite all his problems. Mary is very good in the way that she helps to look after him.'

'I think I hear our menfolk doon the stairs. I'll get the maid to bring us some more tea,' Margo said.

Flora chuckled. 'Aye, there's no mistaking my John's great booming voice.'

John and Richard joined their wives in the living room for some tea and cakes. David was in the corner, propped up on cushions. Although he moved his head from side to side, his eyes did not fix onto anything and rolled about in their orbits. Occasionally he would make noises that seemed to suggest that he was aware of his surroundings, and he would get excited when anyone approached and spoke to him. Richard and Margo often wondered what thoughts, if any, went on inside his head.

After a lot of chatter about families and also the news from London of the dreadful murders perpetrated by the person that they were calling Jack the Ripper, inevitably the conversation turned to their disabled children.

'Have ye thought about what happens when David gets to be an adult, Richard?' John asked.

'How do ye mean?'

'Well, will ye be able to look after him like ye do now?'

'What other option is available? He is our son, and if it is God's plan that we should have a child who demands our close care, then we will provide it. Don't ye think that about your William?'

'Aye, we do,' John replied, looking across at Flora. 'But we have wondered if there are any institutions where he would get care, if we were not around.'

'Have ye ever paid a visit to one of these mental asylums, John? They are dreadful places where disturbed people are dumped because their families are embarrassed to have them around their homes. I am sure that ye have had comments made to ye about William being a stain on the family? Margo and I have certainly had them. One dreadful woman asked Margo what crime we had committed that God should punish us with an imbecile child. It is guid that I was not there, otherwise I would have found it difficult to restrain my temper.'

'I suppose, living on the farm as we do, we get fewer visitors,' John said. 'When we do get visitors we put William away in the bedroom upstairs. I suppose that we are embarrassed rather than ashamed, but we have never considered putting him in an institution. It worries us, though, what will happen when we pass on. Who will look after him? He may be not right in the head, but he seems perfectly healthy in his body. He may live to an old age.'

Margo spoke up. 'We have just got to work from day to day and not worry too much about the future. We have seen medicine improve so much in our lives. Hopefully that will continue and better help will be available for David and William.'

'Aye, well, on that note I think that we need to get back to the farm, John,' Flora said. 'It will be milking time soon.'

Margo nodded. 'Your boys will be taking charge of matters on the farm soon. Flora was telling me that Andrew had taken a real interest in the coos and helps oot with the milking, John.'

'Aye. He's turning into a real dairy man. He can tell me the name of each coo and their sire and dam,' John noted with a touch of pride. 'Tom's more interested in the arable side of the farm and the horses. He's planning to enter the ploughing contest in the autumn.'

'Well, there ye are, John. Two extra workers on the farm to reduce the wage bill that ye are always moaning aboot.' Richard chuckled.

John and Flora left their friends and made their way back to Garclaugh. They were both quiet on the journey as they pondered their conversation with Richard and Margo and considered the future for their son William.

*

Two days later, whilst everyone at Meikle Garclaugh was busy, a pony and trap came down the drive into the farm. Flora looked out of the steamed-up window of the kitchen and tried to identify the man and the young girl who were climbing down to stand in the yard.

'Now, who's that who has come in?' Flora said to Jean, the maid. She wiped her hands on a towel and removed her apron. She brushed her hair back and went out of the door from the back place into the yard, where she immediately recognised James Stevenson.

'Good day, Mr Stevenson, and welcome to Meikle Garclaugh,' Flora greeted her visitors.

'Good day, Mrs Baird. Please call me James, and this is my daughter Barbara.'

'Och aye. John told me that you might visit. Will ye come in and have something to drink? I'll send Jean to tell John that ye are here.'

The visitors were taken into the kitchen, where Flora put some milk into a pan and found the tin where she kept the biscuits that she had made.

'Here, Barbara, have a biscuit. I'm sorry that I can't offer you some cake, but with five laddies in the hoose, cake doesn't last lang.'

'Thank you, Mrs Baird.' Barbara said in a confident voice. Flora looked more carefully at this pretty, self-assured girl. Her study of Barbara was disturbed by shouting outside in the yard, followed by a stamping of feet as a figure ran past the kitchen window. The back door burst open and wee John ran panting into the back place.

'Wheesht! Just slow down, wee John, we have visitors,' Flora said in as loud a voice as she felt was polite in front of the guests. 'Now take your boots off and come in here.'

John removed his boots and sheepishly came into the kitchen.

'Now, this is Mr Stevenson and his daughter Barbara.'

Wee John looked from his mother to the man who was standing by the window and then the girl who was sitting on one of the kitchen chairs. She was holding a bonnet in one hand and a biscuit in the other.

'Good afternoon, Mr Stevenson. Good afternoon, Barbara,' he responded with his best mannered voice. He looked up at his mother. 'Can I go now?'

'No, you can stay and talk to Barbara till yer faither gets here.'

John's shoulders dropped and he gave an audible sigh. Flora sent him an admonishing stare, which made him stand up straight, rather fearful of what he might hear from his mother after the visitors had left.

The door of the back place opened and John's father appeared in the doorway. 'Ah, welcome to Meikle Garclaugh, James,' he exclaimed. Then, on spotting Barbara, he added, 'And welcome to you, young lady, and what might be your name?'

'This is Barbara. She is my youngest daughter,' James responded. 'She was getting in the way at home, so I thought that she could join me and see something of the northern side of the Nith.'

'Have ye never been over to the best side of the river?' the elder John asked, chuckling. 'Then yer in for a treat.' He turned to wee John. 'You can tak Barbara around the steading when I am showing Mr Stevenson some of the bulls.'

After the visitors had finished their drinks, they left the house and walked across the yard to the back of the cattle sheds, where the bulls were kept in pens. James Stevenson immediately took an interest in the Ayrshire bulls that were in the pens, unlike his daughter, who was taking more interest in another pen with some calves staring dolefully through the wooden slats. Wee John led Barbara across to the calf pen and climbed up onto the wooden rails.

'These are the young bull calves that will go to market soon to be sold. They are pure Ayrshire and come from the Garclaugh herd, so they'll make a lot of money,' wee John announced proudly. He began to swing with one hand on the top rail, but lost his grip and, waving his arms wildly, fell backwards onto the muck and straw on the floor of the pen. Barbara put her hand to her mouth to try to suppress her laughter, whilst John struggled to his feet and examined his wet and stinking trousers and shirt. He looked through the rails at Barbara and wanted to say something, but the embarrassment of the situation struck him dumb. Even the calves seemed to be laughing at him.

'What are you doing in there, John?' his father's voice asked. 'Get oot and get yerself cleaned up.'

As John climbed out of the calf pen, his sister Mary appeared and introduced herself to Barbara. The two girls walked off alongside the byre towards the orchard, leaving John to wander back to the house to change his clothes. His mother was not impressed when he appeared in the back place smelling of cow dung.

'What a state, wee John! What will young Barbara be thinking of you? Now strip off yer dirty clothes here and go and get yerself cleaned up. Ye'll need to wash yer hands in the sink.'

Wee John took off his dirty shirt and trousers and left them in the back place. He went across to the sink and used the new water pump that had recently been installed. The cast-iron pump had been connected to the well, which was alongside the entrance track just beyond the yard. It allowed the family to pump water directly into the kitchen sink, instead of relying on buckets of water having to be hauled up and brought across to the house. The housemaid thought it was a wonderful invention, as did Maggie, the dairy maid, who needed lots of water for cleaning all the cheese-making equipment.

Wee John could hear the voices of the men downstairs in the kitchen, and by the time he appeared with clean clothes, James Stevenson and Barbara were outside and climbing back into their trap. Clearly business had been sorted. John was pleased that he did not have to show his embarrassment to young Barbara again.

CHAPTER NINETEEN

May 1890

At last another girl had been born at Meikle Garclaugh. Christina, named after John's mother, Christina Clark, had been born on the 22nd of March 1889. Mary, who was now eighteen years old and had almost given up hope of a having a sister, was particularly excited. She had helped her mother with Chrissie during her first year and was now helping her sister take her first steps.

It was coming up to Whitsun, and the Thursday before was when the Castle Races took place. The Castle Races had been held in New Cumnock for a hundred years, although originally they were a horse race down the main street in Castle. They had since grown into a May fair, with many hawkers' stalls and entertainment booths. By 1890 they had also become an opportunity for local rivals to show their prowess at various sports, including running, boxing, quoiting and even hammer throwing. As the mining community had grown over the years, so had the size of the fair, with many miners taking an unpaid holiday to attend.

Most of the Baird family were going to travel across to Castle Green for the fair, so the shooting break was full as they set off. Chrissie was sitting on Mary's lap, alongside Gilbert and Hugh, who did not have to go to school that day. Mr Wales, the new headteacher, had chosen to close the school rather than face a losing battle to get the children into classes. Wee John sat up front on the driver's seat with Tom, whilst Andrew remained at the farm with his father. Wee John had given up trying to persuade his brother to allow him to drive. Tom insisted that as the eldest brother it was his right to take the reins, which, considering John was only thirteen and the break was fully loaded, was probably the right decision.

As they travelled along the road towards Mansfield, they could see some of the tents and stalls of the fair set up on the green, next to the

River Afton. By the time that they reached Pathhead there were a lot of people on the road, walking, on horseback or in carts. Children were excitedly running around, with some pulling their parents' arms as they strained to get to the fairground. At the Nith Bridge, the family could hear the buzz from the fairground and Gilbert and Hugh were fidgeting around on the bench to get a better view.

'Just sit doon, the pair of you; we'll get there soon enough,' their mother told them.

On the other side of the bridge she told Tom to stop the shooting break. 'We'll just walk from here, Tom, otherwise ye'll get caught up with all the crowds.' The family descended from the break and Tom turned it around to return to the farm. He would bring it back later with his father and Andrew.

The Bairds joined the trail of other families who were heading into Castle. Flora greeted various mothers who she knew from church, whilst Gilbert and Hugh met up with class friends who were bent on having a grand day out. Wee John was due to leave school soon; although it was no longer compulsory for him to be at school, his father wanted him to stay on until the harvest began. However, many of his school friends, including Walter Steel and Will Howatt, had already left school and were working full-time. Will Howatt was working on his father's farm, whilst Walter had got work as an errand boy at one of the shops in the town. John was hoping that he would meet up with them during the day.

The road through Castle had been transformed by stalls and booths that had been set up along each side. There was barely room for a horse to get through, let alone a cart. The shouts and laughter from the hundreds of people crowding the street bounced between the walls of the buildings, adding to the cacophony of noise. Chrissie clung tightly to Mary's neck and tried to hide her face from the clamour.

The Castle Green had mainly been set up for the games competition, with a large area roped off as a performance arena. At one end were a variety of rides with brightly coloured structures, tents and flags. John and Hugh were keen to have a ride on one or two of them, so Flora gave them some pennies to pay for some rides. The two boys ran as fast as they could down the lane that led towards the green and the various rides, although this meant pushing their way through the crowds that had grown around booths at the entrance to the green.

At one large tent the boys paused to listen to an announcer introducing the man standing on the platform next to him. The announcer was dressed in a long red coat and wore a bright cravat around his neck. He had a wide moustache that had been lacquered to a point at each side. The man next to him looked as if he were wearing a set of long woollen undergarments, with a leather belt around his waist.

'Any man who can last three rounds in the ring with Jim McKenzie will go home with a guinea in his hand. Who's up for the challenge?' the announcer shouted across the crowd.

The boys did not wait to find out if anyone was going to take up the challenge; they ran on to the fairground rides. They had spotted a stall with swinging boats and had both decided that they would go on this ride first. They paid their money and climbed into one of the wooden boat-shaped seats. Each boy sat facing the other and could hold on to a rope that hung from the wooden pole suspending the boat. When they alternately pulled on the rope the boat began to swing, and the harder they pulled the higher the boat swung. It wasn't long before the boat was swinging violently from one side to the other, but, as hard as the two boys tried, they could not get the boat to go any higher. Eventually the stallholder told them their turn was over and the boat was gradually slowed to a halt. The boys staggered out onto the grass, giggling with delight.

Meanwhile Flora, Mary and little Chrissie were wandering along the stalls that were selling all manner of hats, parasols and bonnets. Mary was keen to buy a nice bonnet but knew that it would be pointless asking her mother, as Flora did not approve of wasting money on such vain items. They had also called into the new Co-operative shop that had opened the previous year in a building at the bottom of Castle, towards the Nith Bridge. This novel shop had been started by two coal miners, against opposition from some in town, but it seemed to be doing good trade on this day, particularly from the miners' families who were keen to support 'their' shop.

Flora spotted her good friend Margo with her family, so they headed in their direction. 'Hello there, Margo,' Flora announced as they approached.

Margo turned and smiled. 'Good day, Flora and Mary, and how is wee Chrissie?'

Chrissie smiled at Margo, then buried her face again in Mary's shoulder.

'How's your Annie?' Flora asked.

Margo turned to look across at a very pale and sad-looking girl who was standing behind her, then spoke quietly to Flora so that her daughter could not hear. 'She has her good days and her bad days, but she was determined to come out to see the fair today.'

As if prompted, wee Annie lifted a handkerchief to her mouth and coughed a racking cough that made her bend over and wince with obvious pain. She slowly straightened and then continued to look around at the stalls, as if dealing with tuberculosis were just one of the things that she had to endure. Margo put her hand out and stroked the hair at the back of her daughter's head. Annie looked up and smiled at her mother, before commencing with some more coughing.

'Has Richard been able to give her anything to help the coughing?' Flora asked.

'We give her some medicine to help her sleep at night, but if she takes it during the day it makes her so drowsy that she can hardly walk. We don't want to dope her up so much that she can't get outside into the sunshine.'

'Poor wee mite,' Flora whispered, touching Margo's arm to register her sympathy.

The athletics competition were starting in the main arena, so they made their way down the lane to Castle Green and found some benches that had been provided for spectators. There they stayed watching a variety of athletics events. One event was called 'hop, step and jump'. Everyone was keen to see if another youngster would copy the spectacular achievements of Tom Proudfoot, who could jump tremendous lengths. He had even managed to jump across the railway station platforms. But despite all their best efforts no one could get close to the records set by Tom and his amazing legs.

The running races were next on the programme, and an announcer asked for the competitors for the under-sixteen running race, which was four times around the field. A track had been marked out with small flags on poles. About thirty runners lined up behind a tape held by two of the officials, waiting for the starting gun. Flora, Margo and the others saw the smoke shoot out of the gun and a second later heard the report, which echoed from the large gasometer at the gas works behind them. The group set off in a bunch running alongside the River Afton, which formed the eastern boundary of Castle Green. The bunch soon spread out as the serious athletes overtook the occasional runners, who had set off far too fast and were now out of breath and slowing. As the group approached Flora and Margo, Chrissie started to cry, so Flora turned around to take her from Mary's arms, just as the runners were passing the bench where they were seated.

'Isn't that your John, Flora?' Margo asked.

Flora turned to study the runners, but it was Mary who confirmed that it was John in the leading pack. 'Aye, that's wee John.'

'What does that boy think he is doing?' Flora asked. 'He's wearing his best breeks and goodness knows what he has done with his shirt, because that vest he's wearing is not his.'

'He's doing all reet, though, Maw,' said Mary, who was now standing and cheering on her brother. By the time the group came around for their second lap, Flora had got over her initial anger and was also cheering on her son. Unfortunately, despite the support from his family, John trailed in well behind the serious runners. He was met at the finishing line by Hugh, who gave him back his shirt, as he put his hands on his knees and tried to recover his breath.

John managed to avoid his mother for most of the morning, in fear of a severe reprimand. The two brothers used up the rest of their pennies on the coconut shy and the shooting gallery. As lunchtime approached, however, the pangs of hunger made them seek out the rest of their family.

It was their sister Mary who eventually found them. 'Maw has gone over to the doctor's hoose with Mrs Robertson and Chrissie. Maw wants you to go over there for lunch, as Mrs Robertson has invited you both.'

'But we want to stay at the fair,' whined Hugh.

'We don't need to stay long,' John said. 'Come on, I will race you there.' So John led Hugh in another running race, leaving Mary to shout after them to wait for her.

*

'So what made you want to enter the running race, John?' his mother asked when he finally arrived at the surgery apartment.

'Walter Steel was already entered and he said that he was a better runner then me. The only way to prove that he was wrong was to enter the race as well.'

'And did you beat him?'

'Aye, of course I did. I've always beaten him in running races,' John replied.

'I think it is in Proverbs that the Bible says that pride goeth before a fall. I'll ask yer faither; he will know.'

'It was just a wee race, Maw.' He knew that his father was likely to give him a long lecture from the Bible about boasting.

Once the Baird and Robertson families had devoured most of the food from Margo's pantry, the youngsters streamed out of the apartment: all except wee Annie, who had retired to her bed after the strains of walking around the fair in the morning. Margo decided to stay with her, whilst Richard accompanied Flora, Mary and the children back to the fair. John and Tom were due to come over from the farm and meet up with the rest of the family, so Flora wanted to stay down on the green by the arena, which she had agreed would be the meeting place.

As they walked towards Castle they could hear the raucous shouts and laughter from the men who had already consumed a lot of ale at the long tables set outside the Castle Hotel. The owner was doing his best to earn as much as possible during Castle Races day, even if it meant that there would be crowds of drunken miners and inevitable fights. Flora was glad that Richard steered them all safely past Trotters' shop and down the lane to Castle Green. Richard was treated with great respect by the miners, so, drunk or not, they would not cause him or his family any bother.

It wasn't long before John and Tom found the two families sitting together. They had found themselves a spot where they could watch the five-a-side football matches that were due to take place between various local teams. Tom was due to play for Afton Thistle, so he had come with his kit and a pair of boots. Some of his team even had proper football boots with studs, but most, like Tom, played in their working boots.

The first match kicked off with quiet and restrained spectators, but once the drinkers at the Castle Hotel realised that the matches had started, they came down to support their miners' team and the volume of cheering and verbal abuse increased noticeably. Tom's team had won their first match and now had to play one of the miners' teams from Connel Park. Tom was a strong man, but he looked small beside some of the miners in the opposition team. At the starting whistle, their centre forward rushed towards Tom, who had the ball, and kicked his legs from under him. Tom ended up on his back with the large miner dribbling the ball away down the field towards the goal.

'Come on, referee, that was a foul,' Tom shouted to the retreating back of the referee.

The rest of the match continued with an increasing number of blatant fouls until, inevitably, a fight among all ten players erupted. Various officials, fathers and miners ran onto the pitch, some to try to break up the fight and some to add to the mayhem. The referee blew his whistle constantly, with no reaction from anyone. Eventually he threw it on the ground and walked off.

After about five minutes the players started to back off from each other and the spectators wandered back to their places. A new referee took up the challenge of trying to continue the match. He warned all the players about foul play and reminded them that the whole town was watching. Fortunately he managed to get the match to a conclusion without any further confrontations, although the Afton Thistle team lost.

Tom came across to his family sporting a black eye. Richard examined it and told Tom that there did not seem to be any serious damage, but that he would need to put a cold wet cloth on it to reduce the swelling.

John was not at all impressed by his son's behaviour. 'Half the toon was watching you all brawling like drunk miners on a Saturday night. You're a Baird; don't let doon the name.'

'I wasn't the one who started the brawling. I was just defending myself.'

'I saw what was going on. Now keep well away from those lads in case they want to start it up agin.'

'Aye, I will. I don't want to add to my bruises,' Tom replied, carefully touching his swollen eye.

Wee John and Hugh were quite impressed by their older brother's performance during the brawl.

Since Tom had no further matches, it was decided that the Bairds would all go back to Garclaugh. They gave their farewells to the Robertson family and made their way to the smithy on the edge of town, where they had tethered the horse and break. They gave a coin to the stable lad who was looking after the horses and set off, leaving behind the noise and excitement of the Castle Races fair.

CHAPTER TWENTY

June 1890

The May fair stalls had been packed away and the excitement of the event was already starting to become just a memory. However, the working life at Garclaugh continued. The grass in the river meadows had been cut and had dried well in the sunny days that followed. The family were busy collecting the hay and loading it onto the carts to be stored as winter fodder for the animals. The hay had been raked into long lines across the field, using a horse-drawn hay sweep, so now Tom and Andrew were busy forking the hay onto a cart. It was a Saturday, so wee John and Hugh were there to help as well. John was holding the horses steady and moving them forward alongside the line of hay, whilst Hugh was on top of the cart trampling the hay down so that it was more compacted.

Eventually no more hay could be put onto the cart, so John led the horses towards the ramp at the top of the field that took the track over the railway lines. The horses always got twitchy going over the railway, as they could feel that the surface was strange beneath their hooves. The lead horse stopped on the lines and John pulled on the reins to get the horses to continue moving forwards. It was at this point that he looked along the valley to see the tell-tale column of steam that showed an approaching train. He pulled at the reins with greater force and picked up a stick from the side of the track to give the horses some more encouragement.

'There's a train coming, John,' Hugh shouted from his perch on top of the load of hay.

'I ken. I'm just trying to get them to move o'er the rails,' John replied, with a hint of panic in his voice. He took hold of the bit strap to pull the lead horse forwards, but its eyes were rolled back and staring at the approaching train with its plume of white steam billowing into the air above the engine. Instead of pulling forwards, the horse started to walk backwards.

'John, the train's coming, move the horses!' Hugh bellowed.

John took the stick and raised it above his head to bring it down on the lead horse's back. However, the lead horse saw what was about to happen and decided it was time to move forwards after all. It began to move its feet, but the second horse was still stationary. After some uncoordinated pulling and shoving, eventually both horses strained forwards on the traces that connected them to the cart. The cart swayed alarmingly but started to move off the rails. John continued to pull and yell at the two horses and the cart lurched towards the safety of the farm track.

Unfortunately, the swaying movement of the cart caused the load of hay to shift sideways and it began to slip off the cart, along with Hugh. With nothing to steady himself except the loose hay, Hugh began to fall sideways. He waved his arms wildly in the air and managed to twist his body in an effort to break his fall. He landed on his front, directly on top of the sharp ballast between the rails. The fall winded him and he lay dazed, struggling to breathe. He could hear a shrill whistle and gradually he realised that it was coming from the train that was now bearing down on him. He looked up and found himself staring at the front of the engine only a few yards from him. There was nothing that he could do but lie flat with his arms stretched in front of his head, as the engine and the train rolled over him.

He screwed his eyes closed and pressed his face into the ballast stones between the rails. The sharp edges of the stones pushed into his skin and he could smell the oil from a hundred trains that had passed over the spot where he lay. The engine wheels creaked on the rails and Hugh could feel the wooden sleepers move slightly as the huge weight of the steam engine pressed down on the rail on either side of him. Hot water dripped onto him from the pipes and valves that led to the hissing pistons, which drove the huge driving wheels. Hugh felt a blast of heat as the firebox passed a few inches over his head. He was aware of a flash of light and he opened his eyes to see the gap between the engine and the leading carriage. He was tempted to lift his head but then remembered the heavy chains that he had seen hanging from the couplings, when he and John had watched trains trundle past at a much safer distance. He knew that one of these chains would crack his skull as easily as a breakfast spoon would a boiled egg.

Rather absurdly, he began counting the wheels that flashed past in front of his face. One, two, three, four, then a flash of sunlight. Another four and another flash of light. On and on the train travelled, until suddenly there was a blaze of sunlight and the squealing noise of the wheels grew more distant. The train was gone and he was still alive.

John was unaware of what had happened, as he was trying to steady the horses down the sloping track and get them away from the train, which was now flying past behind the cart. The loud whistle from the engine had disturbed the horses even more and it took all his strength to stop them bolting.

'Wow! That was close, Hugh,' he shouted up at the cart once the horses had settled.

Meanwhile Tom and Andrew had been watching the drama unfold from where they were standing in the hay field. They both gasped when they saw Hugh fall from the cart onto the track. They ran towards the crossing, reaching the bottom of the slope as the last carriage passed over Hugh. Neither spoke as they anticipated a most horrific scene. As they ran up the slope Hugh raised his head above the rails, looked around and let out the breath that he had been holding in whilst the train moved over him.

'My God, Hugh, you're alive!' Tom shouted as he reached the top of the slope. 'Are ye hurt?'

'Aye. Well, no. Except my chest and face hurt where I landed on all this ballast,' he replied in a rather stunned manner.

'Ye've just had a train going over the top of ye and all ye can say is that yer face hurts. Ye lucky, lucky beggar!' Tom laughed, joined by Andrew, who was similarly relieved to find their wee brother still alive.

John was unaware of how close Hugh had come to a gruesome death. He had tethered the horses and had run back up the slope to find Tom and Andrew brushing off Hugh's clothes and inspecting the scratches and red marks on his face.

'Ach, don't worry, Hugh,' Tom told him. 'You'll have some fine bruises and a lot of aches, but all things considered ye'll have quite a tale to tell the laddies at school.'

'What happened, Hugh?' John asked. 'I thought that you were still on the cart.'

'Nay. He dropped off and decided to find out what the underside of a train looked like,' Tom said, chuckling, to John's amazement. 'Go on, you two, take the cart back to the steading.'

Hugh walked gingerly towards the cart, holding his hand to his face. John walked beside him with more questions than Hugh was able to answer. When the boys reached the cart, Hugh turned to John.

'Next time, let's look up the line and check that there is no train coming.'

*

It was later in the summer that the sad news of Annie Robertson's death came through to the farm. It was not a huge surprise as Annie had been getting weaker and weaker over the preceding weeks. Flora had tried to visit Margo as much as possible, but with the haymaking and the start of harvest, it was not easy to get away from the farm. They had seen the Robertson family at the church on Sundays, but recently the family had usually arrived late and left early.

Richard had taken on an assistant, a young Canadian called Donald Noble. Although he was not a fully qualified doctor he had relieved Richard of a lot of his workload, so that he could spend more time with Annie. Richard was racked with guilt that he could not do more for his daughter. He had read medical journals to get the latest research on this dreadful disease that was sweeping the country. There was a theory that it was being spread from infected cows through the milk, which was now being shipped to cities by the trains, but there was still no effective treatment. Good food and fresh air seemed to be the most popular recommended treatment, a treatment that Richard and Margo had tried to provide in abundance, but without any improvement in Annie's condition. The old name for tuberculosis was *consumption*, and it certainly felt to the family like little Annie was being consumed from within by this dreadful disease.

The funeral was held at the town church and officiated by James Millar. The Reverend Murray had fully retired and moved to a house in Cumnock, so it was too far for him to come to services in New Cumnock. Any funeral for a child is a sad affair, but the arrival of the small coffin in church brought sobs and tears to the eyes of the congregation, as well as to the family members. John and Flora had never seen Richard looking so disconsolate, and after the funeral was over they returned to Garclaugh, thankful that they had never had to bury one of their children.

CHAPTER TWENTY-ONE

September 1891

Come autumn, so pensive, in yellow and grey,
And soothe me with tidings of Nature's decay.

'My Nanie's Awa', Robert Burns

It was a cloudless and cool evening in early autumn, and wee John and Hugh had managed to get away from the farm. They had crossed the Mansfield road and were now heading up the slope behind the cottages towards Upper Linn, where they intended to call in on the lime kiln workers. John had visited them a couple of times previously with his friend Mungo Sloan and now wanted to show Hugh.

The lime kilns were operated as part of the Mansfield estate and were quite a large operation. The lime from the Mansfield kilns was particularly good for making mortar for constructions that were to be under water, like bridge foundations. As the road and railway network in South West Scotland was expanding there was an increasing demand for this lime, so the kilns were operating at full capacity.

Each kiln consisted of a large stone building with a bowl-shaped hollow at its centre. These would often be built into the slope of a hill. The bottom of the bowl had a hole, called the eye, which opened into a smaller arched space below. The eye was about half a metre in diameter and had an iron grill at its base. The grill was hinged and could be reached from the arched space below.

The bowl would be packed with alternating layers of limestone and coal until it was full to the top. A fire would then be set in the space below the kiln, so that the flames heated the coal through the iron grill and ignited it. The coal in the whole batch would then catch a light and heat up to a very high temperature, until the calcium carbonate in the limestone changed into calcium oxide, or quicklime. Once all the coal had burned and the mixture had cooled, the grill would be hinged open and the contents of the kiln poked out of the eye and sifted to remove the unburned limestone. This left a pile of quicklime, which was very caustic and would burn the skin, particularly if it was wet. Great care was taken to make sure that quicklime was kept out of one's eyes, where it could cause permanent damage.

Although quicklime was used for making mortar, Sir Charles Stuart Menteath had initially spread it on the land of his estate to sweeten the soil by reducing the acid. It was this innovation that had improved the soil and increased the yields of corn and grass.

The Mansfield estate had a number of lime kilns and limestone quarries. Before the railway had come, when the roads were still rutted tracks, Sir Charles had constructed a tramway to take coal, limestone and quicklime to Sanquhar, where they were loaded onto larger wagons and barges to take them down to Dumfries and beyond. This proved to be a valuable source of income for the estate. The smoke from the lime kilns could be seen for many miles and on some windless days it mixed with the smoke from the coal mines, creating an acrid smell that seemed to taint the whole Nith valley.

John and Hugh crept through a bank of trees that formed the boundary of the lime kiln area. They could see about four workers around the base of the kilns, some sitting illuminated by the orange glow from the fires, whilst two inspected the fires and poked the burning logs with long iron poles. Feeling emboldened, the two brothers left the cover of the trees and walked slowly towards the workers. When they reached the edge of the working area they stood quietly watching the men.

One of the older men, who had been poking at the fire and adjusting a sheet of steel that helped to control the air reaching the flame, turned around to take up his seat with the other workers. He spotted the two boys standing in evening gloom.

'Hello. We have a couple of spectators. And who might ye twa be?'

'I'm John Baird and this is my brother Hugh. We are from Garclaugh Farm,' John answered confidently.

'John Baird, eh? You had better keep well awa from the kiln, then; we don't want you disappearing into nothing like the other John Baird.' The workers, some smoking long clay pipes and others drinking, chuckled. 'Come closer, then, boys, and tak a seat. My name's Rob Giffard.'

John and Hugh joined the workers seated on a large log. The heat from the fire under the kiln was very intense here and the boys had to shield their faces with their hands.

'Dinnae fret, boys; ye'll get used to the heat in a while,' Rob Giffard assured them, taking his place next to the other men.

After a short wait John plucked up courage to ask the question that he was desperate to ask. 'Who's the other John Baird you spoke of?'

Rob Giffard looked across at John and smiled. 'Ah, now there's a tale. The other John Baird worked up at Cumnock at the Benston Limeworks. One evening he went to check on how well the limestanes at the top of the kiln had cooked. He put his foot onto the stanes on the top to test how much of his weight they would hold. But he didnae realise that the top layer of stanes were suspended like a bridge above a cauldron of hot quicklime. As he put more of his weight onto the stanes they collapsed and he fell into the kiln, with a great spout of flames shooting up from the fire below.' Rob Giffard threw his hands into the air to add some drama to his storytelling. But John and Hugh were already entranced by this gory tale and stared open-mouthed at him, awaiting the rest of the story.

'Well, the other men could only stand in horror, because the heat from the kiln was so strong that they could not approach any closer. John Baird had completely disappeared, like a tortured soul being sucked into the depths of hell.' Rob paused for more dramatic effect. 'When they came to empty out the quicklime the next day, there was hardly enough of his body left to put into a cigar box, let alone a coffin.'

He paused again and all the men were silent for a while, before one of them spoke.

'Now at his labour. In a moment gone. To all a warning, who behold this stone.'

'What's that supposed to be?' asked one of the others.

'It is written on his gravestane at Cumnock kirk. I used to visit it when I was a laddie and my brother told me the story,' the man responded.

'So, young John Baird, ye should heed the warning and keep well awa from these kilns,' Rob Giffard said. 'Now, awa with ye back to yer hoose. It's getting dark and yer mither will be wondering where ye are.' He pointed away into the gathering darkness. John and Hugh quickly stood up and ran away towards the trees through which they had crept a little earlier. The men around the kiln laughed at their fast exit.

As Rob Giffard had predicted, Flora was outside the house calling the names of her missing sons. After a little wait she could hear their footsteps running down the drive. John and Hugh appeared from around the byre wall, running into the light from the house windows.

'Where have you twa boys been? I've been calling for ages.'

'Sorry, Maw, we went for a walk to Mansfield and lost track of time,' John answered.

'Lost track of time? You don't need a watch to see that it was getting dark. Now get inside and have yer supper before yer brothers decide to eat it for themselves.'

The two brothers scuttled into the back door of the house, ducking as they ran past their mother in case she decided to dispense a whack to their heads. Their father and elder brothers were still sitting around the dining table.

'Where have you twa been?' their father asked.

'We just went for a walk to Mansfield and it took us longer to walk back than we expected,' wee John answered.

There was a pause whilst their father considered this, but it was Tom who spoke.

'I know where they've bin. You've bin to the lime kilns, haven't ye?'

But before John could protest their innocence of this accusation, Hugh blurted out, 'We only stayed a short time.'

'Well, ye should not have stayed any time at all,' their father said. 'It is not safe around those kilns. Grown men have got hurt up there, and once they start drinking alcohol on the evening shifts it is even more unsafe. I want you to promise that ye will not go up there again.'

Both boys spoke together. 'Sorry, Paw. I promise.'

John looked across at his elder brother Tom, who was smirking at him. John tried to give him a look of contempt, before his father spoke and broke his stare.

'Now sit yerselves doon and eat yer supper.'

Tom and Andrew left the dining table, leaving John and Hugh with their father. John told his father of the story that Rob Giffard had related about the John Baird who fell into the hot kiln. It was a story that his father had heard told many times before.

'Was that John Baird a relative of ours, Paw?' wee John asked.

'Well, he lived at Polquhaup Farm up by the Black Loch and I have heard it told that my grandfaither or great-grandfaither farmed at Polquhaup. So it is possible that the John Baird who came to such a dreadful end was a distant relative. But there are plenty of Bairds living in the county and they are not all relatives. Now awa ye go and get ready for bed. I hope that story disnae gie ye nightmares.'

TWENTY-TWO

October 1891

Thou saw the fields laid bare and waste
And weary winter coming fast.
And cozy here, beneath the blast,
Thou thought to dwell
Till crash, the cruel coulter past
Out through thy cell.

'To a Mouse', Robert Burns

Later that autumn the Baird family prepared to travel up to Cumnock for a ploughing match, in which Tom was going to compete. Tom and Andrew had already set off early with the two Clydesdales that were going to do the ploughing. One horse was hitched to a farm cart, into which the plough had been lifted, whilst the second horse was tethered behind. Tom had spent the previous day grooming the two horses and plaiting their manes. He had also polished a set of brass ornaments that would be fixed to the various traces and harnesses on the horses. Not only did he want his ploughing to be of a good standard, but like all the competitors he also wanted his ploughing team to look their best. There would be a variety of prizes for the ploughing, but there would also one for the best-turned-out pair of horses.

His cousin James, from South Blairkip, was also going to be competing, as were other Baird relatives from around Sorn. It would be quite a gathering of Bairds and a chance to share their news.

Flora was not keen for Chrissie to have to spend the whole day in a cold field at Cumnock. In fact, Flora was not very enthusiastic about the trip at all. She had managed to persuade John that the ploughing match was an event for the men and boys, rather than the womenfolk and wains. She was also worried about William, as the new maid whom they had recently employed to help look after him was proving to be very unreliable. So it was wee John, Hugh and a young Gilbert who joined their father in the shooting break to travel to the farm where the ploughing match was due to take place. Flora had packed them some bread and cheese for the day, along with a couple of flasks of water.

The field was very crowded when John and his sons arrived in mid-morning. They unhitched the horse and tethered it to a stake that John hammered into the ground. He was puffing hard by the time he was finished and he had to lean against the break to catch his breath. John had been noticing this breathlessness over the preceding months and wondered if he should speak to Richard about it. But, like many men, he decided not to make a fuss.

He rounded up the boys and they left the horse to graze, in order to find where Tom had been given a strip to plough. They soon spotted Andrew, who was waving at them from further down the field.

Tom had already completed several long furrows and John looked along them, with one eye closed, to check that the furrows were straight

Ploughing at Darnay Farm.
Photograph courtesy of Margaret Smith

and of the correct depth. He was pleased with what he saw and felt a surge of pride in what his eldest son had achieved. He turned to Andrew. 'That's a grand start he has made; let's hope he continues. Have you seen anything of yer Blairkip cousins, Andrew?'

'Aye. James from South Blairkip drew a strip over by yonder trees. It's not a great draw as the ground is quite stony up there, so he might struggle to keep the blade in the ground. Charles from North Blairkip has got a strip back towards where you left the horse. You walked past his lot.'

John turned and shaded his eyes to look towards where Andrew was pointing. The North Blairkip Bairds were relatively distant cousins of John's, but he knew them well, having grown up on the neighbouring farm.

'Aye, well, they've all grown up since I last saw them. They were just boys when I was over there last. I'll go over and greet them later.'

'They are a superstitious bunch. They streeked the plough afore they started,' Andrew said with a chuckle.

'There's nothing wrong with continuing auld customs, Andrew. If they believe that it brings them luck, then what's the harm?'

Streeking the plough was an ancient custom that went back hundreds of years. In order to bring good luck and to please the fairies that were believed to live in the soil, the plough was given food and drink before the blade was put into the earth. The food was traditionally bread and cheese and the drink was, of course, whisky. The food was wrapped in a parcel and tied to the beam of the plough, whilst the whisky would be poured over. The ploughman would usually take a dram of the whisky as well. Although not many ploughmen still chant the ritual rhymes when they reach the end of a furrow, many farmers still insist that the first furrow to be ploughed after the harvest should be done on a Saturday and should be preceded with this ceremony of bread, cheese and whisky.

Tom eventually brought the horses to the end where his father was standing watching him. John gave his son some encouragement and told him that he was doing a grand job. He then began to add various pieces of advice, which Tom noticeably ignored, just replying, 'Aye,' and continuing to turn the horses.

The distance that the horses pull the plough is called the furlong, a shortening of *furrow long*. A furlong is 220 yards. This is the distance that a pair of oxen, or horses, could pull a plough continuously without needing a rest. At the end of the furrow, as the horses were turned around ready for the next furrow to be ploughed, they would get their short rest. The judges noted how well the competitors lifted the plough out of the soil at the end of the furrow and then how well the ploughman would put it back into the soil at the start of the next. The 'ins and outs', as they were called, were to be in a straight line along the headland and not ragged.

John's nephew, Jack, from South Blairkip, walked down to where his uncle and the boys were watching the ploughing.

'Good morning, Uncle John. I hope that ye're well.'

'Aye, I'm well. And how are all yer kin up at Blairkip?'

'Quite well, thank ye, Uncle John,' Jack replied, then, after a pause, 'although Faither seems to be finding getting older a struggle.'

'How do ye mean, Jack?' John asked, turning to look more closely at his nephew.

'Well, he gets very confused these days and then lashes oot at everyone. The other day he couldn't remember where he had put the key to the strong box and was getting angry that someone had stolen it. We eventually found it in his coat pocket.'

'Aye, well, that's getting older, Jack. Ye'll get there one day.' John was trying to make light of the situation, but he could tell that Jack was worried. He decided to change the subject. 'How's James getting on up at the top end of the field? Andrew told me that it is quite stony up there.'

'Aye, it is stony, but the judges will allow for that. He seems to be making a reasonable job of it. Your Tom is doing well; those furrows look as if he has used a string line to keep them straight.'

John turned to look along the furrows to which Jack was referring. 'Aye. He's doing a good job. We hope that it impresses the judges as well.' John's speech trailed off as he looked over Jack's head and beyond to a couple of men who seemed to be handing out leaflets to the spectators. They were not dressed like farmers; in fact they looked more like businessmen. 'Now, who are those men and what are they doing?' he wondered aloud.

Jack turned around to look. 'Oh, they're some government men. They're handing out leaflets about farming in Canada, Australia and New Zealand. They're advertising for ploughmen to work on the farms o'er there. They are even offering to pay the passage for good ploughmen.' Jack put his hand in his coat pocket and pulled out one of the leaflets to let John read it.

After a little while John gave a huff and handed the leaflet back. 'Well, we certainly don't need to lose oor good ploughmen. There is enough talk about farmers packing up and taking up farms in Canada.'

'We learned aboot Canada at school, Paw,' wee John added to the discussion. 'There are thousands of acres of land waiting for farmers to go over there and farm it.'

'Is that so?' John replied. 'Do you fancy going over there yerself, then?'

Wee John didn't reply, but in truth the idea of travelling to another country far away did excite him. He had often looked at the map of the world and traced his finger across the sea to Canada, and had spun the globe on the teacher's desk to find Australia on the other side of the world. He knew that there would be few opportunities at Garclaugh, being the third son in the family. Perhaps he could become a farmer somewhere in the Empire.

*

After the initial excitement of arriving at the ploughing field, the day began to drag for wee John, Hugh and Gilbert. Various farmers had come over to talk to their father as they watched Tom complete more furrows. Wee John became more interested when he heard the menfolk talking about the Prince of Wales opening a wonderful new bridge over the Firth of Forth at Edinburgh.

'It's the most wondrous structure I have ever seen!' one farmer exclaimed. 'It is a true wonder of Queen Victoria's reign. Thousands of great tubes welded together into two huge mountains of metals, and through the centre runs the railway track, fixed in place by all this steel.'

'Well, you widnae get me travelling o'er it,' a second farmer said. 'Look what happened to the Tay Bridge just twelve year ago, with hundreds killed.'

'It wasnae hundreds killed. It was a lot, but nae hundreds,' a third interjected.

'I think it were aboot seventy,' the first farmer said. 'But this new bridge is a far better bridge than the Tay Bridge. It will still be standing in a hundred years.' He continued to extol the virtues of the Forth Bridge, eventually pausing when it was clear that his audience's attention had turned back to the ploughing match.

The elder John broke the silence. 'Aye, these are extraordinary times in which we are living. New machines seem to be invented every few months. It's possible we're going to be using one of these new steam-powered threshing machines at Mansfield this autumn. The new factor has been talking aboot hiring one for us to use on the farms.'

Wee John had been listening to the discussions and vowed that he would do his best to find a way to see this wondrous new bridge, but was more excited about the idea of a steam-powered threshing machine coming to Garclaugh. He went over to pass on the news to Hugh and Gilbert, who were busy throwing clods of soil at each other. Neither of the younger boys really understood what wee John was trying to explain, but they could tell that it would be exciting from his description. All three then decided to start a soil-throwing competition, which ended when their father gave them a severe bark and one of his 'you dare let the Baird name down?' stares.

Tom eventually finished ploughing his strip and set about unhitching the two Clydesdale horses from the plough. The horses were covered in sweat and were foaming at the mouth from where they had been chewing at their bits. They stamped their large hairy feet on the ground after their exertions on the plough. Andrew took one of the horses and began to rub it with a hessian potato sack that they had brought with them for that purpose, whilst Tom did likewise with the other. They then led them down towards a water trough that had been set up, and both horses had their fill. Andrew gave them each a food bag with oatmeal and molasses as a reward for their hard work and left them tethered.

The results of the judging would be given soon, so Tom and Andrew walked back up the field to the area where the judges would announce the awards.

Tom won second prize for ploughing for the 'straightest best manner with a pair of horses abreast, a third of an acre in under three hours, not less than five inches deep'. John felt that Tom should have won, but the first-placed ploughman worked for the Marquis of Bute, who had donated the medals, and John was convinced the judging had favoured the Marquis's man. There was no point in making a fuss and the family returned in good heart, pleased that Tom had demonstrated his ploughing skills to the farming community.

Wee John suggested that a photograph should be taken of Tom and his medal. He had meant the remark somewhat sarcastically, as he was jealous of the attention that Tom was getting. Their father, however, thought that this would be a grand idea. He announced that he would call on the photographer in town and arrange for him to come out to Garclaugh and take a photograph of the family.

It was the following week when the photographer arrived and set up his tripod and camera in the yard, in order to take a picture of the whole family. That is to say, nearly the whole family. William, of course, would not be appearing in the photograph. Flora was not that keen on the idea of having her photograph taken, but knew that it would be pointless protesting when John had made up his mind.

The photographer arranged the family in a group with John and Flora seated in the centre and the rest of the family standing around them. Chrissie was told to stand at the front, but standing stationary is not easy for a two-year-old, so the photographer had quite a task to get her to be still whilst the camera lens was open. Eventually he was satisfied that he had got a good picture and packed away the camera. When he visited the farm two days later, with a print of the family group, John was very pleased with the result, although Flora was less well pleased.

'I look old in it, John. You cannae show that photograph to oor friends.'

'But oor friends see you all the time. What difference does it make that it is a photograph?'

'Do you mean that I look this old all the time?' Flora exclaimed with horror.

John was flummoxed. Should he tell her that the photograph was not a good likeness, in front of the photographer, or admit that she did look older than her years? In the end he decided to be diplomatic.

'Of course you dinnae look old. These photographs don't always give a good likeness.' He turned to the photographer, who was about to protest that the camera did not lie, and gave him a silencing stare. 'We will have some prints of this photograph, perhaps three. Can you put one in a frame with glass?'

As the photographer was about to leave in his horse and trap, John asked him whether he would be able to take some pictures of his bulls. John was keen to advertise his herd and had realised that photographs could help him to do this. His bulls and cows were continuing to win awards at cattle shows and the reputation of the Garclaugh herd was growing. It was time that he spread the reputation of the herd further afield, especially as he had heard that livestock dealers were paying good prices for good Ayrshire bulls and cows to ship overseas to Canada, Australia and America. Despite the poor situation for many farmers in Scotland at that time, Garclaugh was not just managing to survive but was making a good income.

The Baird family. Centre: John and Flora. Children, clockwise from left: John, Thomas, Mary, Andrew, Hugh, Gilbert, Chrissie

CHAPTER TWENTY-THREE

October 1894

The country approached the end of the century and the sixtieth year of Queen Victoria's reign. The previous decade had brought a change in the attitude of the ruling classes to the working classes. The desperate plight of the working classes had become somewhat of an embarrassment to an increasingly wealthy country, and model villages were being planned to improve the living conditions for the workers in factories. This philanthropic idea had been pioneered in Scotland at the New Lanark cotton mills, where Robert Owen had not only constructed tenement blocks for workers, but had also built a school and encouraged his workers to take evening courses to better themselves with education, rather than drink themselves into oblivion with alcohol. A young David Livingstone benefited from these opportunities, although as a child he would still have had to share one room in the tenement block with his brothers and sisters.

At the collieries in New Cumnock there was increasing pressure to satisfy the demands for coal for the growing industries in Glasgow and beyond. At the Bank Collieries the young William Hyslop had improved the management of the pits since his father's death. The collieries were modernised and working hours were cut, following the positive mood of the times. However, when a downturn happened towards the end of 1894, wages across all the mines in Scotland were cut by a fifth. This brought about the first national strike in Scotland, which lasted fifteen weeks. As union funds and contributions from the public dried up, so did support for the strike.

Farming was also going through a difficult time. The price that farmers were getting for their wheat was only a third of what was being offered forty years previously. Many farmers were losing their tenancies because they could not afford the rent and some were moving south to England or, if they still had some savings, to Canada. So there were hard times for both those who worked on the ground and those who worked under the ground.

Parochial boards had been set up in Scotland to administer poor relief. An Inspector of the Poor was appointed to ensure that funds collected from local taxes for the poor were only given to deserving cases. In New Cumnock the inspector was Alexander Moodie, and John Baird's uncle John had been one of these inspectors for the Sorn area. Poorhouses or workhouses had also started to appear in Scotland, with one being built in Ayr in 1860. As the population of New Cumnock grew, so did the demands being put on the parochial board. With regular fatalities in the mines, the widows and orphans of the dead miners often ended up being helped with board funds.

Richard Robertson and Gilbert Sloan were both members of the New Cumnock parochial board. However, they had very different attitudes to the poor and the distribution of parochial board funds.

The two men were once again at loggerheads at a board meeting. Richard was trying to keep his temper under control as he answered an outrageous remark from Gilbert Sloan.

'The poor dinnae want to be poor! They dinnae want to have to come to us and beg for money. Most of the people we are considering this evening are poor through nae fault of their own. Look at William King, who injured his leg in that mining accident at Burnside pit; he was just dumped on Mr Moodie's door by the colliery managers. He was their employee, injured in their mine, and he should have been their responsibility.'

'That's just one exceptional case,' Gilbert retorted. 'In most of the cases that we consider the folk are either idle or stupid and expect us to bail them out of the situation that they have got themselves into. Just look at the mess the miners' unions created with that strike. We had the families begging around oor doors for food and, worse, stealing food from the farms. If they had not gone on strike, then they widnae have been desperate for food.'

'It was the cut in wages that made them desperate, which is why they had no choice but to strike,' said Richard, becoming increasingly angry.

'There's always a choice, but why should the rate payers have to help them when they make wrong choices?' Gilbert demanded.

Robert Howat, the chairman, butted into the argument. 'Gentlemen, gentlemen. You have made these points to each other many times afore and ye ken that ye're nae gaing to agree with each other. Let's move on to the next agenda item afore ye resort to yer fists.' He paused to allow Richard and Gilbert to calm down. 'Now, the next item is very unusual. You will be aware that William Arthur, who used to farm Wellhill, I believe, has left £10,000 in his will to be distributed to the poor. He has stipulated that he wants half sovereigns distributed every Whitsun and Martinmas to seventy of the parish's poor. It's a huge amount of money that he has left. I met him a few times and he didn't strike me as such a wealthy man; in fact he always seemed to wear auld and patched clothes.'

'That's how he became wealthy, by not spending his money,' another member of the meeting added, to the amusement of everyone.

The meeting went on to discuss how the generous gift would be invested and distributed. Gilbert Sloan proposed various investment schemes, which mostly seemed to connect with his or his family's businesses. Fortunately his proposals were so obviously inappropriate that they were rejected in favour of a straightforward savings account at one of the larger banks, such as the Royal Bank of Scotland.

Once all the board's business had been concluded Richard picked up his coat and left quickly to avoid having to spend time close to Gilbert Sloan. As he paused outside the town hall to put on his coat, Alex Moodie joined him.

'You mustnae let that dreadful man get ye so riled, Richard. Ye ken that he does it deliberately?'

'I ken. I ken. But I cannae let him get awa with such outrageous statements at a public meeting. Ye are right; he does do it to rile me. I can see the smirk on his face when I react.'

'How are things at the rows with the typhoid? Is it abating at all?'

'Aye, we have had fewer cases in the last week. I have managed to persuade the collieries to provide clean water, and they are also giving the miners more coal to help them boil all their drinking water. But it has been a bad business. A lot of wains have died. All the families are weak, having had such poor food during the strike. With the winter fast approaching, a typhoid epidemic is the last thing that the miners and their families need.'

'Aye, there's going to be many widows appealing for poor relief. We could do with some more benefactors like William Arthur. Perhaps we should ask young laird Hyslop to make a contribution to the poor fund?'

Richard chuckled. 'I wish you luck with that plan, Alex. Anyway, I must get back for my supper. At least you have an easier walk home now that they have got the gas lighting working.'

Alex Moodie turned and looked up the road towards Castle, where he could see the light glowing from gas street lamps that had been erected on one side of the road. 'Aye. It's another modern innovation that has come to oor wee toon. Will these wonders never cease?'

'We are living in a time of great wonders, Alex. Did you see the weather forecasts that they displayed at the post office during harvest? Amazing that they can predict when it is going to rain two days in advance. Let's hope that we get a mild winter this year and keep everyone healthy. I bid you a good night.' Richard turned and walked down the road towards Bridgend, where his family were waiting in the new house that he had had built, just beyond the Old Mill.

*

Mary had been struggling to help her mother with the housework at Garclaugh. Some months previously she had found a lump in the lower part of her groin and, although it did not give her much pain, it was a concern. As it was in such a delicate area of her body, she did not want to say anything to her mother and she hoped that it would eventually sort itself out. Unfortunately the lump got bigger and more painful.

One day Flora noticed Mary wincing as she was bending down to help lift up William and insisted on having a look at the lump that Mary told her had grown. Flora could see immediately that it was not normal and arranged for Mary to be seen by Richard at his surgery. Mary, of course, was not at all keen to be examined by a man, particularly one who was a friend of the family, so Richard arranged for his nurse to do the initial examination. He pronounced that it was a hernia and that it would need to be fixed with an operation, otherwise it would grow and could cause the bowels to be squeezed and become infected. He told Flora and Mary that he would make the arrangements for the operation with the hospital in Ayr.

A couple of weeks later John returned from a visit to his family at Sorn. He had wanted to see his brother Tom, who was starting to suffer from senile decay. Since Tom's wife Elizabeth had died two years previously John was keen to give the family support. John had also called in to meet with Robert Wallace at Auchenbrain Farm, just outside Mauchline, to discuss buying a cow from his herd. The Auchenbrain herd was seen as being one of the best Ayrshire herds in Scotland and John was keen that the Garclaugh herd should match its reputation.

John came into the back place and stamped the mud off his boots, before removing them. Flora heard him coming in and greeted him as he came into the kitchen. 'You're back, then. Come and warm yerself by the range.'

'Aye. I got a lift from one of these cabs that they have brought to the station. I thought that they were mad to introduce them in New Cumnock, but it was very comfortable and not too expensive.'

'Wheesht! Those fancy Glasgae things. I'm surprised that they have survived all the bumps and holes in oor country roads.' Flora paused and looked at John. 'So, what news from Blairkip?'

John removed the last of his outdoor clothes and stood with his back to the range and his hands clasped behind him. 'Not good. Not good at all. He's a shadow of his former self, Flora. He thought that I was oor faither. When I tried to explain who I was he got angry and started shouting at me and calling for Elizabeth. Helen and Maggie are doing their best to look after him, but he is a big man and when he starts one of his angry fits, they can't hold him. His lungs are not good either. He started a coughing fit whilst I was there and he did not sound at all good.'

'Aye. Well, none of your brothers are getting any younger.'

'Maggie was telling me that Helen's fits are getting more frequent as well. Maggie is afeared that she is going to do herself some harm if she falls and cracks her head on something hard.'

'Have they been to the doctor with her?' Flora asked.

'The doctor wants to tak her to the hospital in Ayr, but Helen doesn't want to go,' John explained.

'What does young Tom say aboot it? He's the head of the hoose now.'

'Tom agrees with Helen. He says that they have dealt with her fits throughout her life and they will continue to do so.'

'Aye, well, he's probably right, but if she gets worse then they will have to do something. He's a good lad, Tom,' Flora said. 'I just hope that he finds himself a wife and settles doon.'

'Ah, well, that's the other piece of news. Tom has found a wife; he's getting married to Maria Wilson, the dairy maid, in December. He's hoping that we can make it up to the wedding.'

'What day in December?'

'Wednesday the fifth.'

'Aye, well, it's the least we can do,' Flora said. 'Perhaps we can take the young ones, Gilbert, Hugh and Chrissie. It would be good for them to meet some of their cousins. Are they having a spread at the farm after the service?'

'I dinnae ken. I didnae ask.'

'I'll send a message and tell them that we will come up the day before. I can help them with the food.'

CHAPTER TWENTY-FOUR

December 1894

With joy unfeigned, brothers and sisters meet,
And each for other's welfare kindly spiers.

'The Cotter's Saturday Night', Robert Burns

John, Flora, Gilbert, Hugh and wee Chrissie travelled up by train to Mauchline on the day before nephew Tom's wedding, as Flora had arranged. They were collected at the station by Jack, who took them on to South Blairkip. It was early December, but an unseasonably warm wind blew from the Atlantic. However, Flora had brought some extra clothing for Gilbert and Chrissie, because she knew from experience that South Blairkip was a cold house.

Maggie greeted them as they climbed down from the break, with Helen at her side. 'Welcome, Uncle John and Aunt Flora. We are glad to see you all. And welcome, wee Chrissie. Why, you were just a bairn the last time we saw you, and look at you now; you're a young lady.'

Chrissie squirmed under the unwanted attention from her cousin.

The family were ushered into the house and were greeted by a blast of heat coming from a large fire in the front parlour.

'That's some fire you've got in the grate. I can't remember it being so warm in here,' Flora remarked.

'We try to keep it as warm as possible for Faither. When he sits all day without doing any exercise he gets so cold.'

'He's no better, then?' John asked, looking across at his brother slumped in an easy chair in the corner of the room, illuminated by the orange glow from the fire.

'No. The doctor says that he has given up and will drift away from us now.' Maggie spoke quietly. 'He barely recognises us. He speaks to me as if I were Mither. I used to correct him, but it's easier for us all if we just go along with whatever he believes.'

Flora moved towards Maggie and gave her a big hug, causing tears to run down Maggie's cheeks. 'You are a wonderful daughter.' She turned to Helen, who was standing close by. 'And you too, Helen.'

The darkness arrived quickly, and as soon as supper had been consumed Flora put the children to bed. She needed to talk to her nieces about the plans for the next day and what food they needed to prepare.

Her husband went into the front room, where his brother was still sitting in his chair. Young Tom and Jack were also sitting at a small table on the far wall, away from the fire. John took a chair and moved it closer to where they were seated.

It was young Tom who spoke first. 'So, Uncle John, I hear that the Garclaugh herd is going well. I met with the stockman from Auchenbrain recently and he was saying how you and Rob Wallace have been sharing bulls.'

'Aye. We got some grand young stock coming on. We've a three-year-old bull called Substance for whom we hae high hopes. He has blood from the Castelmain herd. It'll be a while afore we can get up to the standards of the Auchenbrain herd, but we'll keep trying.'

The room returned to silence, with just the crackling of the fire and the heavy breathing of Tom in his fireside chair.

'So what plans have you two got for the future?' John asked. He was referring to a time after his brother had passed away. Although he didn't state this, the two brothers understood.

Young Tom answered first. 'Well, I will carry on here, now that our tenancy is secure. I've been running the farm for the past couple of years anyway. James is at West Montgarswood Farm, so hopefully he will make a good job over there.' He turned towards Jack. 'I hope that Jack will stay on to help here, until he can find his own farm.'

Jack looked at his brother, then nodded in a non-committal way.

'This should be a happy time for your marriage, Tom,' John said. 'It's a shame that you have had to take on all this extra burden of running the farm and keeping the family together.'

A voice came across the room from the corner where Thomas senior was in his chair. 'Marriage? Who's getting married?'

The two brothers stood up quickly and went across to their father.

Young Tom bent down to speak to him. 'It's all right, Faither. I'm getting married tomorrow. Do you remember meeting Maria the other day?'

'Aye. I remember. She's the dairy maid. Makes grand cheese.'

Tom laughed. 'Aye, that's right, Faither. She makes grand cheese.' He watched his father, waiting for him to say something else, but he had fallen back to staring blankly into space.

'He seemed quite with it then, Tom. Does he often do that?' John asked.

'Aye, he sometimes seems to get his memories back and talks sense, but it is usually only a wee burst.' Tom stood up, struggling to hide his mixed emotions of anger and despair. 'I'll need to get to bed. I have a busy day tomorrow.' He bade his uncle and brother goodnight and left them with his father.

After another silent pause John spoke. 'Aye, well, perhaps it's time that we all headed for our beds. Now let's get yer faither upstairs.'

Jack went around to the back of Tom's chair and took hold of his father's arm, whilst John took the other arm. As they pulled Tom upwards he helped them by standing himself. They guided him towards the door and up the stairs. Flora and the girls had already taken to their beds, so the house was soon quiet, apart from the snoring from various bedrooms.

*

Maria Wilson was a dairy maid at Hillhead Farm, which was part of the Sorn Castle estate. The laird, Mr Somervell, had kindly agreed that the marriage could be conducted in the chapel at the castle itself.

It was another warm day as the relatives gathered outside the chapel and exchanged greetings and embraces. The groom's brother James had come over from West Montgarswood and Christina, his sister, had managed to come over from Nethershield Farm with her eldest daughter Lizzie, who was just five years old. The only family member who was conspicuous by his absence was Thomas senior. The family had decided that he was too weak to make the journey.

The service was conducted by the minister from Sorn Church. Afterwards the guests made their way to the home of Maria's father James, where a marriage supper had been arranged. Flora and Maggie unloaded some of the Bairds' famous Dunlop cheeses from the back of the break. The guests were offered hot whey drinks, with the possibility of added cocoa powder, which Maria's father had managed to buy on one of his trips to Glasgow for his work as an auctioneer. Everyone was keen to try this luxury drink that they had only ever read about in newspapers. It was particularly appreciated by wee Gilbert, who gulped down his chocolate drink and then queued for a second helping, until Flora gave him one of her looks and he slinked back to his place on one of the benches. John, however, was not concerned about taking a second helping and took a third as well, much to Flora's disgust.

Eventually the wedding festivities came to an end and the couple made their way back to South Blairkip, where a marriage bedroom had been prepared for them. The rest of the family followed them soon afterwards.

Darkness was quickly settling over the landscape when they arrived back at the farmhouse. Helen had stayed at the farm to look after her father and had made up some supper for the visitors. After the large amount of food that they had consumed at the Wilson home, only the children seemed to be interested in eating. The paraffin lamps were extinguished and the house again went quiet, apart from some giggles and noises from the marriage bedroom.

The next morning John, Flora, Gilbert and wee Chrissie prepared to set off for Mauchline station and their journey to Garclaugh. John bade farewell to his brother Tom, who looked up at him with a puzzled expression. John felt that his brother was aware of who was speaking to him, even though he clearly did not understand what was happening. John was sad to see his brother in such a state. He remembered him as the strong and confident man whom he had admired when he was a laddie.

On their way to the station Jack took them to see the big wheels at the Catrine cotton mill. These huge waterwheels had been constructed in 1821 to provide power for the cotton mills. Each wheel was fifty feet in diameter and they worked side by side in a vast wheelhouse. John and Flora had seen the wheels previously, as they were erected and working before they had been born, but this was Gilbert's first view and he was both overawed and excited by them. Wee Chrissie was terrified and hung around her mother's neck screaming, so Flora had to take her back to the break.

Gilbert's eyes were like saucers when they got back into the break and he asked his father lots of questions that John struggled to answer. 'Do they ever stop turning? What happens if the water freezes? Can fish swim through them?'

CHAPTER TWENTY-FIVE

January 1895

When frosts lay lang, and snows were deep
And threatened labour back to keep.

'New-Year Morning Salutation', Robert Burns

By the end of December the unusually warm weather changed dramatically as the wind drew bitterly cold air from the Arctic. Temperatures started to drop, and as Hogmanay came and went the temperatures dropped even further. The lochs at New Cumnock froze, which gave the Baird brothers an opportunity to exercise their curling skills. Although John had taken to the ice occasionally, his sons were now keen curlers and participated in many competitions against teams from other towns.

As January progressed snow began to fall across Ayrshire and the rest of Scotland. Roads became blocked and even the railway companies struggled to clear the tracks for the trains. But after a decade or more of cold winters the farmers were well prepared with plenty of foodstuffs and hay for the animals.

The snow was a real problem for the shepherds on the hills. As the snow started, many sheep would huddle in dips and behind walls, away from the wind. But the wind would drop the snow into these hollows and behind the walls, burying the sheep. So when the morning light arrived the shepherds would have to struggle through deep snow to find the sheep and dig them out of snowdrifts. Often the only evidence that there were buried sheep under the snow would be small breathing holes, where the sheep's breath had melted the snow enough for air to get through.

In February it got colder still and dropped to low temperatures that set new records. Minus 27 degrees Celsius was recorded in Aberdeenshire. Even the mighty River Thames froze. Water pipes in and around

New Cumnock froze, depriving many homes of water. Anyone venturing outside found it painful to breathe in such cold air.

Wee John was out with a hammer, breaking the ice on the water troughs so that the cows could drink, when his father came over to him.

'You'll need to come out later to do that agin. Once the coos have had their fill and leave the water, it soon freezes over agin,' John explained, clapping his gloved hands together.

'Yer hands are still feeling the cold, then, Paw?' wee John asked.

'Aye. My feet went numb some time ago. I'll need to stand by the fire for a while to get the feeling back. It's a nuisance.'

'I've just aboot finished out here. All the pens have got hay and the horses have been given their mash. Go and get yerself warmed up, Paw.'

'Aye. I saw the postie deliver some letters, so I'll go and see what he's brought.'

John left the byre and shuffled across the yard to the back door of the house. He peeled his scarf from around his neck. His breath had frozen into a pad of ice, making the scarf stiff. John threw the scarf around a hook in the back place and unlaced his boots. As he opened the kitchen door he could feel the heat from the coal burning in the range. Sarah McHouston was busy heating some whey in a small iron pan.

'Ah. Some hot whey, that's just what I need,' John said.

Sarah looked suddenly worried. 'I was doing this whey for William, Mr Baird, but I will put some more in the pan for you.'

'Naw. You go ahead and get William sorted. I'll have some later.'

John pulled a chair across towards the range and removed one of his socks. He began massaging his feet in order to get the circulation back into his toes. Flora came into the kitchen as he was removing the sock from his other foot.

'I wondered where the smell was coming from,' she said, laughing. 'Do ye want me to put some hot water in a bowl for ye to soak them?'

'I'll just warm them by the range,' John replied. 'Or were yer offering hot water so that I wud get oot of the kitchen?'

'Well, it's no the nicest place to have yer smelly feet. Wheesht, yer toes are fair blue. Ye really need to speak to Richard aboot yer fingers and yer toes going so blue when it's cauld. It's no right.'

'I won't bother Richard aboot some cold toes, Flora. I'm sure that he has far more important things to do. As soon as I get them warmed up they'll be fine.' After a short thoughtful pause he continued. 'I expect I'll see him at the parish council meeting on Wednesday, so I'll mention it to him and see if I should make an appointment.'

'There's the post, John.' Flora brought across a collection of letters and small packages. 'There's a telegram from Sorn. It could be from Blairkip,' she said, rather ominously.

John leaned back in his chair and took a knife from the cutlery drawer beneath the kitchen table. He slit open the telegram envelope, removed the thin sheet of paper inside and read it aloud. 'FATHER DIED PEACEFULLY TUES STOP TOM.'

'Oh dear. Well, it's a blessing in many ways, John. He's nae longer suffering and neither are the family. It sounds hard, but ye ken what I mean.'

'Aye, yer right. I felt guilty a while back when I thought that his death would bring relief to everyone at Blairkip, but it was the truth. I lost my big brother many months ago.'

*

As spring approached and the weather warmed up, Mary was admitted to Ayr hospital for her hernia operation. Richard had reassured her that it would be a simple operation and that the surgeon involved was an experienced man who had carried out hundreds of similar operations. Flora accompanied Mary to the hospital, where she would spend a few days after the operation. They were both nervous as they walked up the steps of the hospital and registered at the reception desk.

Mary was taken up to one of the wards and was soon prepared for the operation by a nurse. Much to her surprise she was told to lie on a gurney to be taken into the operating theatre, even though she could have easily walked. The nurse told her that some patients had fainted as they had gone through for surgery, so it was better to lie down. Flora gave Mary a reassuring wave as she disappeared into the theatre.

Mary was given another reassuring word by the nurse before the anaesthetist put a gauze mask over her nose and mouth and put drops of chloroform onto the mask. As Mary breathed in the strange-smelling chemical her vision started to blur and then she felt as if she were floating around in the operating theatre.

To the medical staff all seemed to be going well during the operation and the hernia was repaired without problem. Unbeknown to the surgeon and staff, the anaesthetic had not been administered properly and, although Mary's muscles had been paralysed, her brain was still very much awake. She felt all the pain of the operation, but was unable to communicate this fact to the medical team who were surrounding her. It was only towards the end of the operation, when she managed to let out a groan, that the anaesthetist realised that she was still awake. He administered some more chloroform, but the trauma of lying awake whilst the surgeon cut into her abdomen and manipulated her intestines would remain in her memory and leave her mentally scarred.

The ward sister came to find Flora, who was busy knitting in the waiting room. 'Mrs Baird? The surgeon would like to have a wee word with you in his office,' she said, pointing to an office not far from the waiting room.

Flora looked up, rather surprised and anxious. Why would the surgeon want to speak to her? Was this about the bill for the operation? She packed away her knitting and followed the nurse into the office, where the surgeon was sitting behind his desk in his tweed suit and bow tie.

'Aah. Mrs Baird. Do come in and sit doon,' he said in a too-cheery manner, Flora thought.

Flora sat.

'The operation went well and yer daughter has had her hernia successfully sorted,' the surgeon said. There was a noticeable pause and Flora noticed him looking at his papers as if he were trying to find the right words for the rest of his statement. In fact, this was exactly the case. 'There was a regrettable episode during the operation when the anaesthetic that was administered was not as effective as it should have been. As a result Mary was partly awake during the operation. However, some further chloroform was administered and this problem was sorted. She is now sleeping and should wake up in an hour or so.'

Flora stared at the surgeon as she tried to make sense of what she had been told. 'She woke up during the operation, you say?'

'Aye, just briefly.'

'So when she was awake did she feel the pain of the operation?'

'No, it's very unlikely.'

'But she may have done? Is that what you are telling me? Oh my goodness!' Flora exclaimed as she realised the implications of what had happened. 'My poor wee Mary. Did she cry out, then?'

'No. But we heard her make some noise, which is how we became aware that the anaesthetic was not doing its job.'

'So it was the fault of the anaesthetic?' Flora asked pointedly.

'Well, patients react differently to the chloroform and it may be that Mary needed more chloroform than other patients.' He shuffled his papers and stood up. 'But the important matter is that Mary's hernia has been repaired and she should not experience any more discomfort from it in the future.' He came around the table to Flora. 'Now, I have to attend to some other patients, so if you will excuse me. Staff nurse Williams will take you back to the waiting room, and then as soon as Mary has woken you will be able to visit her.'

Flora sat in silence in the waiting room, absorbing all that she had been told, and dreadful thoughts began to spin around in her mind. What if Mary had been awake and aware of the operation the whole time?

An hour later Flora was escorted to Mary's bed, where Mary was lying with her sheets and blankets tucked neatly around her. Mary was staring at the ceiling with her eyes wide open. She turned her head to look at her mother and tears began to well in her eyes.

Flora sat down on the chair at her bedside and held Mary's hand. 'Hello there, Mary. How are ye feeling?'

Mary did not speak but just stared at her mother with frightened and desperate eyes. Flora immediately realised that her worst fears must have come true.

'Ye poor wee thing. Did you feel much pain?'

Mary nodded and began to sob. 'I tried to scream, Maw, but I couldnae.'

*

Mary was not the same woman when she returned home. She sank into a melancholy and spent long periods of time staring out of the window in silence. She did not respond when members of the family spoke to her, and John and Flora were desperately worried about her. Richard

Robertson explained that it might take some months of patient care before she would recover.

Thankfully Mary did become more responsive, although she was still not back to her normal self. She would often break down in tears and disappear into a bout of silence; at these times it was a struggle even to get her to eat. The family would rally around her and eventually she would emerge from the dark place that had taken her away. The whole family missed the Mary that they had known before she had gone into hospital for her operation.

CHAPTER TWENTY-SIX

June 1897

It was the Diamond Jubilee for Queen Victoria, and New Cumnock was celebrating along with the rest of the country. Castle was bedecked with patriotic bunting to follow the theme set for the celebrations, which was the celebration of the British Empire, as well as the sixty-year reign of the Queen. The weather had brightened up for the day, which was a surprise to many considering the poor year it had been so far. A carnival parade had been planned and many organisations had arranged to decorate their own wagon, whilst children were dressed up by their parents to fit the theme of each. The parish council had decided that there should be wagons representing the various continents and countries that formed the British Empire, so there was an Africa wagon, an India wagon, an Australia wagon and a Canada wagon.

Tuesday 22nd June was a public holiday, although Tom, Chrissie's brother, had remarked that it was no holiday for dairy farmers who still had to milk the cows and feed the animals. Despite the farm work that had to be completed there was still time for the whole family to go into town and cheer on Chrissie on her carnival wagon.

'Doesn't she look pleased with herself on that wagon?' Flora said to John.

'Aye,' John said, as he peered across at the wagon representing Canada. 'Which one is Chrissie?'

'She's dressed as an Indian squaw next to the teepee,' Flora replied, somewhat irritated. 'Did you no look at her costume as I was getting it ready in the parlour?'

'Aye, I did,' he said defensively. 'But it looks different in the sunshine.' He paused. 'What's a teepee?'

'Wheesht, it's the name they use for one of those tents in Canada. If you cannae see yer ain lassie perhaps you need to speak to Richard aboot yer eyesight, as well as yer tingling fingers? There she is waving,

John. I hope that she disnae hurt someone with that axe that she is waving aboot. Where did she get that axe from, anyway?'

'It's no an axe, Maw; it's a tomahawk,' Gilbert explained, before he realised that he had just provided a large clue as to who had given Chrissie the small hand axe.

Flora glared at Gilbert. 'Well, let's pray that the tomahawk does not end up braining someone.'

After the carnival procession was over the wagons made their way down onto Castle Green, where there were food stalls and various entertainments. The parish council had paid for refreshments to be provided for the town and many folk turned out to take advantage of the free food, including the miners' families, who probably needed it more than most. Some residents objected to the miners taking part in the celebrations, especially as some of the Irish miners had often voiced their objection to British rule in Ireland.

John and Flora were part of the official group on the stage when the speeches were being made and the prizes were being given out for the best-decorated wagon and suchlike. Flora had got herself dressed up for the occasion, as she quite liked being seen as one of the community's leading ladies. Afterwards John and Flora met up with James Stevenson, who was now president of the New Cumnock Agricultural Society. The Baird and Stevenson families settled down at a long table in order to enjoy the lunch that had been provided, with John and James discussing cattle breeding and the amount of milk that they were getting from their cows.

Flora was looking around at the passing crowds, wondering what had happened to wee John, as she wanted him to sit close to Barbara Stevenson. She thought that Barbara would make a fine catch for wee John. She spotted him talking to his friend Mungo Sloan.

'John, come and sit with us for some vittles,' she called. 'There is a spare place that has bin left for ye.' She indicated the empty place with her outstretched hand.

Wee John gave his farewells to Mungo and wandered over to take his place. It was only when he was seated that he looked up and found that he was sitting opposite Barbara Stevenson, whom he had watched arriving at the church most Sundays. She was now twenty years old and a strikingly beautiful young woman. John was unusually tongue-tied and found himself staring at her.

Barbara broke the silence. 'So, John, how is the farm going at Garclaugh?'

'Aye, it's going well.' John paused as he thought about what he should say next. 'We've got a grand herd of Ayrshires, as yer faither knows because he has used our bulls.' He struggled to think of anything else, so he fell silent.

Barbara did not really want to talk about cows and regretted mentioning the farm at all. She decided to try another topic of conversation. 'Have ye been to the new Moss theatre in toon yet?'

'The theatre? Naw. It's no my kind of entertainment,' John replied, between mouthfuls of food.

There was a pause as Barbara struggled to think of another topic. Eventually John decided that he should add to the conversation himself.

'Have you heard that there is a large shipment of meat that has been sent over from Australia for the Jubilee, that is going to be given to the poor folk?' he asked, rather proud that he was demonstrating his knowledge of recent news.

'How do they manage to keep the meat fresh all the way from Australia?' Barbara asked.

'Perhaps it was salted, like they have always done,' John replied. 'But I have read that ships are now using refrigeration to bring meat over from New Zealand and Australia frozen. Perhaps this is what they use.'

'I wonder if any of the meat will get up here for oor poor folk,' Barbara said quietly.

Their conversation was disturbed by some loud laughing from their fathers, who were clearly sharing a joke. Barbara and wee John caught part of their chatter.

'... and do they think that this angling association will stop the dynamite fishing?' James Stevenson was asking John senior.

'Dynamite fishing? What's that aboot?' Barbara asked wee John.

'Have ye no heard aboot the miners doon at the Nith on a Sunday? They steal dynamite from the mines, then they throw a lighted stick into the salmon pools in the river. The explosion stuns the fish, which then float to the surface, where they're netted.' Wee John laughed. 'They are forming an angling association to stop this type of fishing. When the laird's relatives go doon to the river with their fancy rods and lines, there are no fish left. What makes it worse is that they spend hoors by the river trying to catch a fish or twa and then some Irish miner chucks a stick of dynamite and goes hame with an armful of salmon. So they plan to introduce rules to the fishing on the river that will stop the miners and their dynamite.'

'It sounds very dangerous. Does anyone ever get hurt?' Barbara asked.

'Aye, it's dangerous. Some chappie blew his hand off last year.' John chuckled.

Barbara winced. John noticed her reaction and decided that perhaps it would be wise to change the topic.

'I've heard that the new kirk organ is going to be working at the next service.'

'It'll be even better once the builders have removed all their platforms and equipment,' Barbara added. 'The dust seems to have got everywhere in the kirk.'

'If it drowns out my faither's singing then it will be worth it,' John remarked, to a guilty giggle from Barbara. She shielded her mouth with her hand and leaned conspiratorially towards him.

'My faither is just as bad. It's a guid thing that they don't sit next to each other in kirk, otherwise it would sound like a couple of bulls bawling at each other.'

John and Barbara struggled and failed to suppress their laughter, causing Flora to turn and look in their direction.

'You twa are getting on well. I haven't heard Barbara laugh so much since you fell flat on yer back in the cow muck.'

John blushed and looked sheepishly at Barbara. 'Maw! I was just a wain then. Don't embarrass me.'

John and Barbara continued their conversation, sharing stories of their siblings and their friends in the farming community. With farms being spread out across the countryside, it was not often that the young folk living on farms got to meet each other. For the sons and daughters of dairy farmers there were regular cattle shows and sales, whilst ploughing matches also provided opportunities to gather and talk.

Meikle Garclaugh and Nether Cairn were close enough to New Cumnock that John and Barbara could meet local young folk at church events and dances at the town hall. Barbara was not allowed to attend these dances very often, being restricted to the odd church dance. John, however, tried to get to these dances as often as he could. He had quite a collection of female admirers, whose mothers were not at all worried about their daughters attracting the attention of a successful local farmer's son.

Chrissie was sitting with Flora and becoming bored with the conversations that were going on around her. Gilbert had finished his food and had gone off to play with some of his friends from school. Flora was talking to Annie Stevenson about Annie's granddaughter, Mary.

'She's just six years old and as bright as a button,' Annie was saying. 'She's got a lovely singing voice, so it's a shame that she is being brought up in the Free Kirk. She would make a lovely kirk singer.'

'What's a Free Kirk? I thought that all kirks were free,' Chrissie interjected.

Annie and Flora laughed and Flora stroked Chrissie's hair. 'It's the name given to yen of the kirks. It disnae mean that ye hae to pay to go to oor kirk.'

'But why is it called the Free Kirk?' Chrissie persisted.

Flora and Annie looked at each other, silently asking who was going to provide a simple explanation for Chrissie. Annie took up the challenge.

'Well, about sixty years ago there was a big argument in the kirks about who should appoint the ministers. Many ministers were appointed by the laird or some other wealthy landowner. But this made many kirk folk cross, because they thought that they should be able to choose their ain ministers. They had lots of arguments and in some kirks the folk walked oot because they did not like the minister who had been chosen for their kirk. Eventually the folk who wanted to be able to choose their ain ministers decided to set up their ain kirks that were free from interference. They decided to call them the Free Kirk of Scotland. So today folk can choose whether to go to the Established Kirk or the Free Kirk. Yer family and my family go to the Established Kirk.'

She paused and looked at Chrissie, who was clearly pondering on what she had been told. Annie could see that another question was forming in Chrissie's mind, so she tried to anticipate it. 'Of course, wee Chrissie, whichever kirk ye choose, ye will still worship the same god. It's just that the folk in each kirk speak to God in slightly different ways.'

Chrissie seemed happy with the explanation and smiled at Annie. 'Thank you, Mrs Stevenson.'

'That's grand,' Annie replied. 'Ye hae guid manners.'

'That's because I'm a Baird. Paw says that we should never let doon the Baird name and always be polite.'

Annie and Flora laughed.

'Aye. Yer faither's right, yer a Baird,' Annie said. 'And ye should ne'er let doon yer family's guid name.'

CHAPTER TWENTY-SEVEN

January 1897

The new steam-powered threshing machine that had been hired by the Mansfield estate was now available for Garclaugh to use. There was great excitement as two teams of horses pulled the two carts carrying the machines down the drive towards the grain barn.

In pre-Victorian times the threshing would have been done by human power, with workers beating the corn stalks with flails in order to dislodge the grain. This was done in the centre of a grain barn, which had doors on each side. Wind was allowed to blow through the barn, so that the chaff produced during the threshing would be blown away, in a process known as winnowing.

The nineteenth-century horse-powered threshing machines had a rotating drum into which the stalks of corn were fed. Horizontal bars on the drums threshed or beat the stalks of corn, dislodging the grain and allowing it and the chaff to fall through grilles. A fan blew air through the grains as they fell through, removing the chaff. The whole mechanism was powered with gears and pulleys that were driven from a large circular driving wheel, around which one or more horses were harnessed. As the horses walked in a circle a connecting shaft transmitted the rotation to the threshing box.

The new steam-powered thresher worked on the same principle as the horse-powered machines, except that the gears and pulleys were driven by a steam engine. The steam engine could produce the power of several horses and did not need a rest for food and water or need extra workers to keep the horses walking.

The horses were unharnessed from the transport carts and allowed to graze in the nearby field. The engineer, who had come with the machine, then set about firing up the steam engine. All the menfolk stood around watching the process, whilst the women and the girls soon lost interest and went back to their tasks in the house and the dairy.

Eventually the steam pressure had risen to a point where the engineer was happy that they could get the machinery working, so he engaged the mechanism and the belt that connected the steam engine to the threshing machine started to move. For obvious reasons the steam engine was positioned some distance away from the flammable straw, so a long belt, stretched at head height, was used to transmit the power from the steam engine to the thresher. Looking at the belt and the spinning gears and wheels on the thresher, John was glad that Gilbert was at school and away from the dangers that the machine posed to curious young lads.

Tom got himself to the top of the thresher, where he could fork the sheaves of oats down the opening that led into the threshing drum. The cart had been positioned close to a stack, so it was easy to toss the sheaves to Tom on the top of the machine. Andrew was assigned this job, whilst Hugh was helping his father collect the grain that eventually fell through into sacks, although, with his father finding himself increasingly breathless, it was Hugh who was doing most of the heaving. Wee John was forking the straw that was ejected from the back of the thresher onto one of the empty farm carts, ready to be taken into a barn.

The threshing progressed well and the whole stack of oats was threshed in a tenth of the time that it took with the horse-powered thresher. Whilst Tom, Andrew and their father were moving the thresher to another stack and the engineer cleaned out the firebox for new coal, wee John and Hugh went to the house for some lunch and clean water to wash the dust from their throats. Flora stood at the back door, insisting that they brush off the worst of the dust and chaff from their clothes before they came into the kitchen. 'Ye'll need to go into the dairy and wash your faces and hands, as they're covered in dust as well.'

Ellen Stewart, the dairy maid, appeared at the dairy door with a bucket of clean water. 'You're not coming into the dairy; I've just washed it all clean. I don't want any muck brought in.'

John and Hugh took turns to scoop up some water in their hands and wash their faces. They turned and stood in front of Flora, awaiting permission to be allowed into the house.

She smiled at them both. 'That'll do fine. In ye go. There's some broth on the table for ye.'

As they came into the kitchen the new young maid Agnes Clark was with William, trying to get him to take some broth. William was strapped into his feeding chair, which restricted his motion. His uncontrolled and violent movements made it difficult to feed him otherwise. Agnes was only thirteen and had been employed as William's nurse and to help Flora in the house. William was not yet used to having a new person around him and was making it difficult for Agnes as she tried to hold a spoon full of broth to his mouth.

'Please take some broth, Willy,' Agnes said quietly to William, aware that she was now being watched.

Wee John came across to them. He bent down and ruffled William's hair. William turned his head towards wee John and smiled.

'Now, Will,' wee John said, 'you let Agnes give you some broth. It is lovely broth. Yum, yum.' He leaned forwards and supped at the spoon that Agnes was holding out. William turned towards the spoon and opened his mouth, allowing Agnes to give him a spoonful.

'There you are, Will. It's yum, yum.'

William smiled up at him again.

Agnes also looked up at John. 'Thank you, John. He's being a bit awkward today. I think he wants to be outside watching the steam engine.'

'I'll have a word with my mither and see if we can tak him outside later.'

The kitchen was soon filled by the rest of the family as they came in for their lunch. The engineer had been invited to join them, but he wanted to stay with the engine, so Hugh was dispatched with a bowl of broth and some bread.

The menfolk were all excited by the ease at which the machine had threshed the stack of oats. They now had many bags of grain stacked in the barn, ready for milling into meal for the horses and the cattle.

'How lang do we have this thresher to use, Paw?' Andrew asked.

'We've got it tomorrow as well, so at this rate we should be able to get four stacks done. The Houstons have got it next.'

'I wonder if the laird will buy one of the traction engines that we saw at the county fair. Then they would be able to pull the thresher from farm to farm and power it,' wee John added.

'Aye, well, we won't get the threshing done by sitting here wondering,' his father said. 'The engineer will be ready for us to get started on the next stack.'

Tom and Andrew, who had arrived at the kitchen table last, grabbed some cheese and bread as they left to continue their work.

Flora was left with a pile of empty plates where her sons had eaten all the food that had been put out. She turned to Agnes and William in the corner. 'Come on, Agnes, you get something to eat, if you can find some more bread and cheese, and I will try and get William to eat some apple.' She went across to her crippled son and stroked his hair. He looked up and gave her as big a smile as he could manage, before his face twitched and his arms waved in excitement. Flora hushed him and offered a slice of apple, which he chewed before dribbling much of it down the large bib that they had made especially for him. Flora would not be allowing William to go outside to watch the steam engine. She was not going to expose William to the eyes, and the likely ridicule, of the non-family men working outside.

*

Amongst the clatter and bustle of the threshing, a box wagon arrived pulled by two horses. This was the type of wagon that was used to transport animals, which was exactly what was being delivered to Garclaugh: an Ayrshire bull from Castlemains Farm. Andrew saw the wagon coming down the drive and exchanged his task at the thresher with one of the men that they had hired. He was standing expectantly in the yard as the wagon drew to a halt.

John also came across to greet the driver. 'Did you hae any problems on yer journey, Angus?'

'Naw, Mr Baird, nae problems,' Angus replied as he climbed down from the seat at the front of the large wooden box that had been constructed on the wagon. He tied the reins to an iron ring that was set into the wall of the byre. All three men walked to the back of the wagon, where they began to loosen the screw fixing that secured the back. The back was hinged at its base so that it could be lowered to form a ramp leading down to the ground.

Inside the wagon an Ayrshire bull was straining its halter and trying look backwards into the light that had suddenly flooded into its wooden cell. It snorted and its eyes rolled, partly in fear and partly in anger.

John gave instructions to Andrew. 'Gae around to the side door and fix this rope to its nose ring, then get ready to loosen the halter rope.'

At the front of one side of the wagon was a small door that Andrew could open to gain access to the space below the bull's head. He followed his father's instructions and tied a rope to the ring in the bull's nose. This allowed them to lead the bull from the wagon and into an empty pen, where Andrew and his father admired the bull that they had hired to serve some of their cows.

'He's a fine beast,' John said to his son.

'He is, Paw, but why can't we use Herd Laddie as our herd bull?' Andrew asked.

'We will; once he is old enough, we will. But we need to bring new blood into the herd, you know that, Andrew. Although we have good stock, we can always improve on it. We will see if this one's offspring will prove to be champions. If Laddie proves to be a guid yen, then perhaps we can sell him to the Americans, like we did with Spottie.'

Garclaugh Spottie.

Garclaugh Spottie had been shipped across to America by Adam Montgomerie, a cattle exporter based in Ochiltree. News had come back from America that she was producing large amounts of milk and that the new owners were hoping that she might become a record-breaking cow. If this were to happen then the Garclaugh herd would increase in value immediately, as breeders across the globe clamoured to buy bulls and cows from the Bairds. The wagon that had brought the bull over from Castlemains Farm would now be used to take Garclaugh Substance, the sire of Spottie, back to Castlemains to help add to their Ayrshire blood stock.

In these times when some farmers were struggling to stay solvent, after several wet and cold years, the extra money that John Baird was bringing into the farm by selling his Ayrshire bulls and cows was valuable. He was keen to be able to help his sons set up their own farms and secure a future for William, because, although William was weak in his head, his body seemed healthy and he could live a long life.

As Garclaugh Substance was loaded into the wagon, John looked appreciatively at his bull, remembering when it was born and the high hopes that he had for it: hopes that now seemed to have been fulfilled.

'Are ye all right, Paw?' John became aware of someone saying. He turned to look at his son Andrew.

'Aye, I'm fine, Andrew. Just hoping that this bull gets back to us in guid condition.'

'I'm sure that that he will. I thought that you were having one of yer breathless spells,' Andrew said cautiously, knowing that his father got quite tetchy when anyone drew attention to his increasing difficulties in working for long periods.

'I'm fine, Andrew,' John replied curtly.

Andrew watched him as he walked back to the threshing machine. He was concerned about his father, who no longer seemed to have the strength and vigour that Andrew remembered of him only a few years ago. But, then again, Andrew himself seemed to be short of stamina lately, and he was only twenty-three years old. A farm can be a tough place if you are not fully fit, as he was now finding out.

CHAPTER TWENTY-EIGHT

June 1900

It had been a dull and wet first half of the year, with unpredictable thunderstorms spoiling haymaking. Life at Garclaugh, as on all farms, had to continue and make the best of whatever weather came its way. Gilbert had now left school, so there were now five Baird boys working on the farm. Wee John and Hugh were looking to how they could leave Garclaugh and rent their own farms. The difficulty would be finding the money to get started on their farm, as well as finding a good tenancy. The two of them were busy digging out ditches, so that they would be clear to drain the fields of water in the winter.

'If Faither could lend me the money for my passage, I would be off to Canada in a shot,' Hugh said.

'Aye, well, I might join you,' wee John said. 'There is no future for me at Garclaugh. Andrew has his dairy herd, whilst Tom is happy looking after the rest of the land. Paw told me last year that he would see us all right and help us get started on oor ain farms. If he wasnae so poorly I wud be asking him for the money that he promised now.'

'He's disnae seem to be getting any better, John. What will we do if he dies?' wondered Hugh.

'He's got years in him yet, Hugh. Dr Richardson will see that he is all right. There are lots of new medicines these days. Isn't that we were promised in all those speeches when we celebrated the new century?' John paused and took up the pose of a politician. He continued with an English accent. 'A new wealthy Britain with jobs and opportunities for all, in this glorious empire on which the sun never sets.'

Hugh laughed at his imitation of Robert Cecil, the prime minister. 'I just want an opportunity to become a farmer in Canada.' He went back to clearing the ditch of weeds and mud.

'Well, there's lots of other places in the Empire. Australia, New

Zealand, even South Africa, now that the war seems to have finished over there,' John said.

'Naw. I want to go to Canada. I have read all the literature and I have spoken to some of the emigrant farmers who were at the Cumnock market, when they came back to buy cattle and horses. It sounds like good land, without the wild animals and rebellious Boers, like in South Africa.'

'There's lots of red Indians in Canada. They could scalp you when you are sleeping!' John teased his younger brother.

'Ah, stop yer blethering, John, and let's get this sheugh cleared,' Hugh retorted.

The war in South Africa had been in much of the news that year. After the defeats and set-backs of the previous year there had been one success after another, culminating in the capture of Pretoria, the capital of the Boer state of Transvaal. When the capture had been broadcast, to great fanfare, at the Castle fair in May, a school holiday had also been announced, which had brought a huge cheer from the children present. The war had also been brought to the attention of the general public by the exploits of Winston Churchill, a young aristocratic journalist, who had escaped from his prison camp and made it back to British-controlled territory.

*

Andrew's dairy herd had continued to grow and to win prizes at local and regional shows. The Garclaugh herd was now recognised by the Ayrshire Breeders Association as one of the top herds in Britain. Since a long while before his father had become poorly Andrew had taken over the management of the breeding of the cattle. He was admiring a young heifer that had been born two years previously. His younger sister Chrissie was standing with him.

'What is her name, Andrew?' Chrissie asked.

'She's called Bloomer. Garclaugh Bloomer.'

'That's a funny name. Why is she called Bloomer?'

'Well, her mither is called Bloomer, Castlemain Bloomer, so I kept that same name so that it was easy for me to remember which coo comes from which mither.'

'When will this coo have its calf?' Chrissie asked.

'She will calve in September.'

'Will the calf be a heifer or a bull?'

'We won't know that until it is born. I am hoping that it will be a heifer and produce lots of milk. But if it is a bull calf, then I am hoping that I may be able to sell it for lots of money,' Andrew explained, with a satisfied grin.

'Why will you be able to sell it for lots of money?'

'Because it has an excellent faither, an excellent mither and an excellent grandfaither. So it should be an excellent bull, which will go on to produce lots of excellent coos that make lots of milk.'

There was a silence that Andrew welcomed. It was broken by a statement from Chrissie.

'I think it will be a heifer,' she said emphatically.

'Well, we will have to wait and see. Come on, let's go and gie Mary some help in the byre. They will be needing a hand to get the coos tied up.'

Andrew walked Chrissie across the yard to the byre, as swallows wheeled and squealed around them, flying in through the open byre doors to deliver fat grubs and insects to their ravenous chicks. The chicks were squashed together in mudball nests that their parents had constructed in the rafters above the cows. The cows, oblivious to the presence of the swallows above their heads, licked the last remnants of oatmeal and molasses from the stone troughs in their stalls. A handful had been put into each trough to coax the cows into their stalls, but the cows found the molasses so delicious that when the gate to the byre was opened they barged into each other to get to their stalls. They bustled along the passageway in a most undignified manner, their udders swinging between their legs, in order to get to their sweet treat. Each cow knew her own stall, and a young cow would get a painful headbutt from her dominant sister if she went into the wrong stall.

A new dairy maid, Jessie Edwards, had replaced Ellen Stewart in the dairy, but Mary was also working in the dairy, now that the herd had expanded. Andrew and Gilbert also helped to get the cows milked, although Andrew was usually engaged in measuring and recording the amount of milk that each cow produced. A top milk cow would be expected to produce over a thousand gallons of milk in a lactation. This was the time, about 300 days, between one calving and her next. Garclaugh Spottie, the cow that John Baird had sold to a farmer in

America a couple of years previously, had produced 2,627 gallons in one lactation: a world record. John and Andrew had made sure that this fact had been advertised in the *Ayr Advertiser*, to encourage other farmers to pay the high price that they were now charging for access to their bulls.

As the cows came into their stalls, Chrissie helped to attach the chains around their necks to prevent them from backing out during milking. Jessie then came around the back of the cow with a bucket of warm water and a cloth, which she used to clean the udder. Once this was done she would sit on a short three-legged stool, lean her head against the cow's hind leg and begin to squeeze milk from the teats into a clean pail. She had been at Garclaugh long enough now that she knew all the cows and their personalities. Some cows needed a little soothing before she would start milking, whilst others were liable to kick out. For a kicking cow Jessie would put her head in front of the cow's hind leg, so that she could feel if the cow was about to kick and could then move the pail and herself out of the way.

'Can I try and milk a coo, please, Andrew?' Chrissie asked.

Andrew laughed. 'Aye, of course you can. Let's find ye a nice gentle coo. Aah, there's Lady Diana; she's a lovely old coo that will not mind ye having a go.'

He settled Chrissie down on a stool with a bucket and explained how she needed to squeeze and pull the teats at the same time. For the first few attempts no milk appeared, but eventually she started to get the idea and milk squirted down into the pail.

'That's the way, Chrissie,' Andrew encouraged her.

'It's hard work. My hands are aching. I dinnae think that I can do any more.'

'Don't fret. I'll finish her off.'

Andrew took over milking Lady Diana.

'One day, Chrissie,' he said as he worked, 'we will use a machine to milk the coos.'

'A machine? Won't a machine hurt the coo if it squeezes with metal fingers?' Chrissie asked.

Andrew laughed at the thought of a machine with mechanical fingers squeezing the teats on an udder. 'Naw, there's a metal tube that fits over each teat, and the inside of the metal tube has a rubber lining that expands and squeezes the teat. I saw one being demonstrated at the agricultural show. But we won't be getting one here for a long time, because they are very expensive.'

'I hope that we get one before I have to do the milking myself, because it will save me from getting sore hands,' Chrissie said, to a laugh from Andrew.

'I'll see what I can do, Chrissie. I'll see what I can do.'

*

The summer months seemed to pass by quickly as the family gathered in all the hay and soon started harvesting the corn. The elder John's health had been getting worse and one afternoon, as he was struggling to put his boots on in the back place, he collapsed onto the ground, clutching at his chest. Grace Coe, the maid, was in the kitchen and heard his gasps.

'Oh dear, Mr Baird. Are ye all right?' Grace asked.

John was gasping and he struggled to speak. 'Get Flora … get Mrs Baird,' he managed to say.

Grace ran off into the dairy where Flora and Mary were working. They soon appeared in the doorway and lifted John off the floor. By this time John was starting to lose consciousness. Flora untied his collar to allow him to breathe more easily, but even though he was breathing in gasps his skin was losing its pink colour.

'It's his heart. Get one of the boys to ride over to the doctor. Quick, Mary,' Flora instructed her daughter. 'I think Andrew is with the bulls behind the byre.'

It was not long before Andrew appeared at the doorway, then disappeared again as he rushed to saddle up one of the horses. Hugh had heard the commotion and had also appeared. They lifted John out of the back place and carried him through to the living room. By now John was unconscious and going blue.

Flora bent over his chest to listen to his heart. There was silence in the room. Eventually she slowly straightened.

'His heart has stopped. He's gone,' she said quietly, as if to herself.

Grace croaked out a sob and put her hand to her mouth, whilst Mary and Hugh stood and stared at the inert body of their father.

*

The family went about in a daze for the next few days. There was plenty of work to be done around the farm, so the boys were able to hide away their emotions in their chores. Flora and Mary were doing the dairy work, so Mary kept an eye on her mother and Flora kept an eye on Mary.

Richard Robertson had come over as soon as Andrew had arrived at the surgery, but all he could do when he arrived at Garclaugh was certify John's death and verify that he had suffered a heart attack. It was not a surprise to Richard as John had been showing symptoms of heart problems for a few years and had been advised to reduce his workload. John had laughed at Richard's advice, but with five sons working on the farm he had realised that he could step back and let them get on with most of the hard physical work. He had found himself doing more planning with Andrew on the breeding of the Garclaugh herd. Now it was up to Andrew to continue the legacy that John had started.

The church was packed for the funeral, reflecting John's respected position in the community. Neighbouring farmers and fellow cattle breeders attended, along with members of the large Baird family that extended up to Sorn and down to Sanquhar. Flora's brother James came over from Back Rogerton Farm with his wife Ellen. The Reverend James Millar spoke for the family and praised John's faith and his work for the church as an elder. He was buried in the new graveyard on the edge of the town that he was proud to call his home. A stream of mourners spoke to Flora and told her how much they had liked and respected John and that he would be greatly missed. Barbara Stevenson had sought out wee John and squeezed his hand in a tender show of sympathy and affection.

During the previous months, as it had been clear that John had a serious health issue, the boys and Mary had inevitably thought about what would happen if their father were to pass away. Tom, as the eldest, was, of course, confident that he would take over the tenancy of the farm. Andrew was now a fixture at Garclaugh, along with the dairy herd that was earning good money for the farm. Mary would remain at Garclaugh with her mother until she got married, although with her mental issues there were doubts as to whether marriage was a possibility for her. John and Hugh had already been considering emigrating to Canada, whilst Gilbert, at fifteen, had not really thought much beyond continuing to work at Garclaugh. Chrissie, at eleven, was too young to have really considered her future. All Flora's children rallied around to support her and to ensure that life at Garclaugh continued, despite the empty chair at the dinner table.

John, now no longer wee John, was looking through the *Ayr Advertiser* some weeks later when he saw an advert for a manager at a farm near Stewarton, in the north of the county. It seemed as good an opportunity as any to get away from Garclaugh and get some experience of farming on his own. He wrote to apply for the position and was invited to travel up for an interview. So a few days later he rode his newly acquired bicycle to the station and took the train up to Stewarton, from where he cycled out of the town to Mid-Buiston Farm. There he met Jeannie and Agnes Hay, the two sisters who owned the farm. Their father had died a few years earlier at the grand age of ninety-three, leaving the farm to his two unmarried daughters. The Hay sons had moved away, one now living in Australia, leaving Jeannie and Agnes to try to manage the farm themselves. The two sisters liked what they saw in John Baird, an enthusiastic and knowledgeable young man with an ambition to prove himself as a farmer. They offered him the job, which he gladly accepted.

He returned to Garclaugh and informed his mother that he would be leaving. It was not a great surprise to Flora, for he had often proclaimed his intention to find a farm somewhere. His father's affairs still had not been sorted, so there was no money to help him acquire a tenancy. This farm management job was an opportunity to earn some money of his own, as well as to prove himself.

The Hay sisters wanted him to start immediately, so John packed his belongings into a trunk and Andrew took him to the station in the cart. It was a fair distance to Stewarton, but the railway had made the journey time much shorter. It would be easy to return to New Cumnock and see his family, as well as the young lady from Nether Cairn who was increasingly in his thoughts. But now a new life at Mid-Buiston Farm beckoned.

John Baird had come to New Cumnock with his new wife Flora and they had raised six sons and two daughters, as well as many fine Ayrshire cattle. It was now up to his offspring to create their own legacies in this new century that brought the promise of many exciting developments.

John Baird 1831–1900.

My Father Was a Farmer

My father was a farmer upon the Carrick border,
And carefully he bred me in decency and order.
He bade me act a manly part, though I had ne'er a farthing,
For without an honest, manly heart no man was worth regarding.

Then out into the world my course I did determine,
Tho' to be rich was not my wish, yet to be great was charming,
My talents they were not the worst, nor yet my education,
Resolved was I at least to try to mend my situation.

Robert Burns

Historical Notes

The story of John and Flora Baird and their family has been described with as much factual detail as I was able to find in birth, marriage and death certificates and in census forms. Various events, such as Mary's mental condition after waking up during an operation and Hugh's dramatic escape after falling from a hay cart under a train, were family stories, on which I elaborated, but without departing too much from the information that I had inherited. I do not know what medical condition took Mary into hospital for an operation, so the hernia is pure speculation.

All the events described in New Cumnock or in the wider world actually took place during the years shown and I used them to form storylines. For instance, the collapse of the Glasgow Bank did bankrupt hundreds of people across Scotland, whilst the huge grass fires in Canada really did cause there to be bright red sunsets and sunrises for many weeks over Britain.

Despite my best efforts to follow historical fact, many of the scenarios include speculation. For instance, I do not know if a stroke was the cause of Sir James Stuart Menteath's demise, only that his death certificate states that he died after 'two days of convulsions'. One possible cause for these convulsions could have been the stroke that I have included in the story. This also applies to some of the other deaths that I have described, including that of John Baird himself, whose death certificate describes his demise as being caused by 'valvular disease of the heart'.

Below I have provided a little more historical background to some of the scenarios that I have created within *My Father Was a Farmer*.

Farm Tenancies

In 1870 a survey of land holdings was completed in Scotland, which showed that 50% of the area of Scotland was owned by just 118 people.

Most of the farms at this time were held by tenants on large estates. Agricultural tenancies were regulated by common law and the terms of the lease reflected the bargaining strengths of the parties involved. Needless to say, the landowner inevitably held the strongest position. Tenancies were entered into for a fixed period of time, which was generally seven or eleven years. At the end of this period the tenant had to leave, if new terms could not be agreed.

During the 1870s, when John Baird was trying to establish Meikle Garclaugh, economic conditions deteriorated in agriculture. This was partly caused by the impact of competition from America when the Corn Laws were repealed and partly due to a series of poor harvests. This led to an intervention by the government to improve the lot of the tenant farmer and the introduction of the 1883 Agricultural Holdings (Scotland) Act. This made provision for a tenant to receive compensation for the value of improvements that the tenant had carried out on the farm during the tenancy. This was specifically to encourage the tenant to maintain the fertility of the land towards the end of the tenancy, by providing for compensation for such things as unexhausted manure.

The crofters in the Highlands were especially vulnerable to the vagaries of their landlords, and during the end of the eighteenth century and into the nineteenth hundreds of thousands were displaced from their traditional homes in order to make way for more profitable enterprises, such as sheep grazing. This period was known as the Highland Clearances and was notorious for the brutal way in which the Highlanders were evicted, often by having their homes burned. Many thousands died of starvation as they made their way to the coast to try to survive by harvesting kelp and mussels. In 1886 an Act was introduced to secure the tenancies of crofters and stop the land clearances, but the Highlands had been changed forever. The existence of so many Scottish societies in countries across the world bears witness to the extent of the forced mass emigration of the Highlanders.

Sir Charles Stuart Menteath and his son James, on the Mansfield and Closeburn estates, were landowners with considerable foresight and worked hard to improve the estates by encouraging the tenants to adopt new farming methods. At Mansfield this meant using lime to 'sweeten' the soil, by reducing its acidity. This made it better for growing cereal crops and potatoes. Sir James also encouraged the use of new grass seeds to provide better grazing for cattle and sheep, as well as promoting better selective breeding. Selective breeding was used to great effect by John Baird and his son Andrew to improve the Garclaugh herd of Ayrshire cattle.

Local Government

The failure of the water board in New Cumnock to efficiently introduce clean piped water to the population may be attributed to the poor decision-making by those on the board. However, it was also symptomatic of the disorganised and archaic structure that existed at a local level at the end of the nineteenth century. Towns, counties, boroughs and cities all had laws and privileges handed down centuries before by various royals. When there were failures, it was difficult if not impossible to place the blame at anyone's feet.

The situation was resolved in 1888 when the Local Government Act was introduced. This Act introduced elected councils at county level and made the offices of lord lieutenants and sheriffs purely ceremonial. A following Act in 1894 introduced a second tier of elected officers within urban and rural districts and also civil parishes. This provided a structure of local government that more or less survives until this time. It may well be that many local councils ended up with the same people making decisions, but at least they were now accountable and failure could be attributed.

By 1867 voters were still only men over the age of twenty-one who owned land or property, but a new Parliamentary Reform Act in that year increased the number of men who were eligible to vote, including many of the miners in the Ayrshire coal fields. This encouraged men like Kier Hardie to enter politics in order to speak for and improve the lot of working people.

The Railways, Milk and Tuberculosis

As the railways expanded exponentially in the second half of the nineteenth century, more and more people found that they had an inexpensive way to travel. In 1844 a law was passed that forced railway companies to provide a covered carriage on at least one train journey per day, for one penny per mile. These parliamentary carriages had to have seats, but other than that were very basic.

Farmers and growers found the new train services ideal for transporting perishable goods to their customers, and the dairy farmers of East Ayrshire were no exception. John Baird took churns of milk to the station at New Cumnock every morning, where they would be joined by dozens of other churns from neighbouring farms for the journey up to Glasgow. At the dairies in Glasgow the milk would be mixed together, then put into smaller containers for distribution around the city.

Tuberculosis is a bacterium that affects cattle and some other animals. It also attacks humans and in particular the lungs, where it slowly destroys tissue and creates the tubers or growths which give the disease its name. Although the disease is not always fatal, those who recover from an infection will often have reduced lung function. Tuberculosis can be transmitted between people through cough droplets or open wounds; however, it can also be contracted by drinking milk that contains the bacteria. Cows with tuberculosis can pass bacteria into the milk that they produce. So if only one cow in a herd has tuberculosis then the bacteria can end up in the churn that is loaded onto the train. Once mixed with the milk from other farms it will then be distributed across a city, infecting hundreds of consumers. Tuberculosis is a disease that has been with humans for many thousands of years, but the advent of train travel allowed it to spread faster than it had ever done previously.

Until the discovery of antibiotics there was no cure for tuberculosis. It was found that if sufferers were provided with the opportunity to rest, eat good food and get plenty of fresh air, they could sometimes fight off the infection. Any sufferer who did recover would have considerable sections of their lung tissue damaged beyond repair. Many sanatoria were established in rural places across the UK as tuberculosis hospitals, including one that was built in the Afton Valley at the beginning of the twentieth century.

The Demise of the Glasgow Bank

When the UK banking system faced near-collapse in 2008 the government stepped in to bail it out. In 1878 there was no government intervention to prevent the City of Glasgow Bank from collapsing, leaving many shareholders facing bankruptcy and destitution. Although the bank's directors ended up in court for their mismanagement of the bank, their sentences were surprisingly lenient considering the misery they had wrought on individuals and businesses throughout the west of Scotland. It was noted that just a couple of weeks previously, a report had described the City of Glasgow Bank as having reserves of £1 million and paying dividends of 12%. When the bank collapsed it had debts estimated at £10 million.

Late Nineteenth-Century Weather Events

The weather in Scotland, as well as other parts of the UK, between 1870 and 1895 was characterised by some exceptionally cold and wet winters. In some places the second-coldest temperatures ever recorded in Scotland were suffered during the winter of 1878/79, and the cold conditions continued right through into the winter of 1879/80. On the 4th December 1879 a temperature of –31°C was measured in Berwickshire and many rivers froze over. It was on the 28th December 1879 that the Tay Bridge Disaster occurred. The cold conditions did not just affect Scotland; it is reported that the whole of Northern Europe suffered dreadfully cold weather, with Dutch waterways remaining frozen for two months.

The winter of 1890/91 started with frosts at the end of November and the ice lasted through to the end of January. In Worcester the ice on the River Severn was so thick that road traffic was able to use the river ice to cross over, whilst the ice on the lake in Regent's Park was reported to be nine inches thick. A similar cold winter in 1895, when an ox was roasted on the Thames ice in London, ended this mini Ice Age.

A consequence of this quarter-century of cold weather for farmers, like John Baird, was that it was difficult to feed their animals over the long winters. Fortunately the advent of the railways meant that fodder could be moved to areas that needed extra feedstuff. Unfortunately this did not always aid poor people, who found that the price of food went up during these cold periods. During 1879 the harvest was wasted and a famine was reported in many parts of Scotland.

Wombwell's Circus

In 1804 George Wombwell, a London-based shoemaker, began collecting exotic animals after purchasing two boas from a ship in the London docks. He showed them around local pubs and made quite an income from them. In 1810 he abandoned shoemaking and opened Wombwell's Travelling Circus, which travelled to fairs across Britain. By 1839 it consisted of fifteen wagons and a brass band. It eventually expanded to three separate menageries that travelled around the country.

Although Wombwell purchased many of his animals from ships, which came to the London docks from all over the world, he also bred animals in captivity. He was the first person to successfully breed a lion in Britain. He named it William, in honour of William Wallace. There is a story that he used it in a lion-baiting event, in which several dogs were used to attack the lion. The event was stopped after William mauled all the dogs.

Wombwell developed a rivalry with another exhibitor, Thomas Atkins. Once, when Wombwell arrived at a fair in London, his elephant died and Atkins put up a sign, 'The Only Live Elephant in the Fair'. Wombwell simply put up a notice with the words 'The Only Dead Elephant in the Fair' and explained that seeing a dead elephant was a rarer thing than seeing a live one. The public flocked to see and poke the dead one. Throughout the fair Atkins's menagerie was largely deserted, much to his disgust.

Corn Laws

The Corn Laws were tariffs introduced in 1815 on imported foods. They were introduced to keep corn prices high, to favour home-grown grain. The Corn Laws imposed very high duties on imported grain and made it too expensive to import grain from abroad, even in times of hardship. The Corn Laws were supported by Conservative landowners but opposed by Whig industrialist and workers. An Anti-Corn Law League campaigned against the laws for many years, until they were eventually repealed in 1846 by Robert Peel.

Kier Hardie

James Kier Hardie was born in 1856 in a two-roomed cottage in Lanarkshire, Scotland. His mother was a domestic servant and his stepfather worked in the shipyards. At the age of ten Kier worked as a trapper down a mine, opening and closing a door that helped to maintain the air supply for the miners in a given section of the mine, in a ten-hour shift. Kier would have been sitting in the dark and the damp, waiting for coal trucks to be rolled along the tram rails. Despite the need for Kier to work in the mine to help support the family whilst his stepfather was away at sea, his mother encouraged him to read and write. Kier later went on to work with pit ponies and become a hewer at the coal face. Through all this time he continued with his education at night school.

Kier became involved with the temperance movement through his local evangelical church. He preached against the evils of alcohol, which gave him practice at speaking in front of crowds. This skill of oratory led him to be elected as a union official by the miners. When the mine owners reduced wages, more miners joined the unions, and in 1879 Kier was elected as the national secretary of the Conference of Miners Unions. He helped to organise a miners' strike in Lanarkshire which, although ending in failure, led to him being invited to Ayrshire to help organise the miners in that region. In 1881 he led a strike demanding a 10% wage rise. This strike also ended in failure, although the mine owners did subsequently raise the wages, fearful of further industrial action.

Kier then turned his hand to journalism, writing for the pro-labour *Liberal Cumnock News*. This gave him a wider audience and he involved himself with local politics through the Liberal Party. In 1887 his efforts for the miners were rewarded when the Ayrshire Miners' Union was formed.

Having become disillusioned with the Liberal Party, Kier put himself up in the local election as an independent Labour candidate. Despite finishing in last place, he persevered and later helped to form the Scottish Labour Party. In 1892 he was offered a chance to stand for the parliamentary seat of West Ham South, which he won. He soon made himself unpopular in the House of Commons when he campaigned for the abolishment of the House of Lords and for women's right to vote, and he even spoke out against the monarchy.

Over the next few years Kier continued, both in and out of Parliament, to campaign for working people. In 1906 the Labour Party was formed, with Kier as its leader, and twenty-six members were soon voted into office during the election of that same year.

A pacifist, Kier was appalled by the First World War and tried to arrange a national strike against the war. His stance was seen as being unpatriotic and he was often heckled when he spoke in public against the war.

He died, following a stroke, in September 1915.

Milton Keynes UK
Ingram Content Group UK Ltd.
UKHW020724260224
438492UK00007B/482